Big Questions, Little Sleep

By

Linda Imbler

ISBN-13: 978 - 0 - 578 - 65576 - 5

Library of Congress Control Number: 2020905967

For Chuck

Who so loved "Dog"

Foreword

In her note, to *Big Questions, Little Sleep*, which is the second edition of her book, echoing Anton Chekhov's words that the role of an artist, is to ask questions, not to answer them, we find this exquisite artist, Linda Imbler, asking one question after another, reiterating that questions need to be asked at all times .
A self- confessed insomniac, she does not rue her insomnia, but, on the contrary, staunchly believes that her sleepless nights have given her ample time to ruminate over the mysteries of life, time and death.
 I have always been fascinated by her poetry, her sensitivity sparkles through every word, her imagery beguiles and her goodness of heart touches.

 She asks, *How will we ever reconcile the Robin Hood aspect of time —that time is both the thief of youth and the giver of memories at the same time?*
 Why does one year slip into another so seamlessly, yet until the year is done, progress seems to be a fleeting thing? It's only in looking back that we see all the accomplishments made. Why do the dead never report back to us? Is it because somehow we have not connected death properly with time?

I read this with great fascination, finding myself agreeing with each question. Yes, one has to keep asking questions – all the time. She concludes her notes in these words, *'as*

definitive as these poems may appear, they still leave
questions or questions on questions. '

The ravaged face,
belies a younger life,
enlivened with friendship,
suitors constant at the door.

Time, time, time,
slow down.
Time leaves us with *hunched backs, toothless mouths, and*
thin-haired pates, depriving us of energetic activity,
ravaging, savaging, pillaging. Was one really young once,
gifted with energetic strides, with suitors constantly
knocking at the door?
She very rightly says that Robin Hood time, creeps
stealthily in the dark robbing one of one's youth, passion,
beauty, energy, yet gives back in some way by way of
faces , conversations and memories .

Yet, he left to me a pile of memories,
faces and conversations.
A pile growing larger each year,
so he does give back to the poor.

 Yes, indeed, with the passage of time, one loses
prodigiously, but gains too – and paradoxically enough, is
enriched by loss, in the form of heaps of memories,
making us realize that even though a ruin, life can be
splendid *in its disrepair.*

Another very touching poem in this poetic repertoire is the poem, *Age Times Ten,* where she talks of a couple from the age of 8, 16, 24, 30, 50, 70 and 80. Her words about their lives at age 70 and 80, left me with a constriction in my throat and a tingling in my eyes, their mutual love through all the periods of their lives, shining through every word.

Age 70

She helped him button his shirt,
although she had arthritis, too.
Age 80
Side by side, they lie and dream together
beneath the grassy green and starry nights.

One of my favorites in this collection is *The Long Lane,* where she very touchingly writes about her *'first tears'* which streaked her childish cheeks when her furry pal disappeared parting at the fork, her *'next loneliness'* when an old woman, while walking this lane, hugged her and then disappeared, bidding her goodbye , then as a young woman , she met a young man , her *'first love'* , and then her *'first grief'* when the man she wed , grew frail and weak and finally parted at the fork in the road of life , eventually leaving her walking the road alone , making her realize that the long lane is now her home , and *'This is the place I belong.'*

In Futuristic Farm (A Prose Poem), she reminiscences about her father's farm, weekend retreat.

A rural, pastoral farm; a house with featherbeds, cots for extra bodies, mowing pastures, riding horses, barbecuing, tire swings and hammocks, homemade ice cream fresh from the churn, happy, slow days and nights, giving the readers a taste of the halcyon days spent in this *little house on thirty-six acres of refuge, outside a small Texas town, accessible only by one narrow, perilous, rutted dirt road.*

Such heartwarming memories! Well, isn't this what life is all about? Chunks of memories, nuggets of warmth, and vignettes of time spent skating, lying in hammocks, playing pranks, swinging on tire swings and then once again , sitting in the swing in the porch in the patio, wistfully sipping coffee, ears pricked to the echoes of *Footsteps That Have Long Faded* .

This awe- inspiring book, not just pulsates with Life, but also throbs with themes of Death. In *Six Feet*, she says,

Even the larger than life get no more than six feet down at the end. There's no volcanic snoring from the sleepers here reposed. No fanatic cackling from those who once lived within now powdery sanatoriums. Jawbones no longer festive or with coy wag, no gummy promiscuity among once social butterflies. There's no loathsome musings, nor clandestine plots against those who stand above in trodden woe.

What an enchanting multi- layered poetic offering this book is- colored in the myriad hues of some frozen and flamboyant moments , fleeting images , echoes of fading footsteps , infancy, youth , old age and the finishing line ,

which we reach holding those memories close to the chest
– a handful of regrets , grudges , grouses and unshed tears .

In *The message of Breath,* she writes with a heart touching
poignance about that first breath announcing with a
cacophony of wails a new birth, eventually leading to the
inevitable death rattle.
The book has many tributes written with a heart- warming
sincerity, some of them are to JFK, [*John, Gone twice: His
message of hope, for prosperity for all, interrupted.*]
Bowie, [*frail, unswerving, death unnerving*], Leonard
Simon Nimoy, Spock of the Star Trek series [*The Search
for Nimoy February 27, 2015]*

A heart made weak on Earth,
now throbs with distant life,
up and out, stellar, sparkling,
continuing, in a part of heaven
of which we cannot conceive.

As the notes of *Every day I have the blues, and Rock me
Baby* wafted across to me, I read her tribute to Riley B
King , aka BB King [the American Singer -songwriter ,
guitarist, [16 September 1925- 14 May, 2015] hanging on
to every word ,as she reminded us , with an incredible
poetic adroitness of *The Blues enduring positivity And
Riley's eternal legacy* and with the poet , I could

Feel the weight and vigor of this genre so aural,
Hear what's reflected in the sonic mural,
Elation, salaciousness, sensuality,
The mortal coil's gravity,

Call and response felt deep in skin and soul,
A beat strong and true, never growing cold, [*Berclair ,We*
Miss You, B.B. King)

In her note to the poem , she says , On May 14, 2015, the
world lost a large part of its heart with the passing of Riley
B. King, known to the world as B.B. Born on a cotton
plantation called Berclair, he practiced guitar endlessly,
later played live (brilliantly) more than that, and influenced
an uncountable number of people. Gentle, hardworking,
talented, and generous, I named my newest guitar after him
and wrote Berclair to honor him.]

The following poignant words from *One Man's Karma*
resonated with me, in a big way because, off and on, I have
also written about such incidents.

A black man lynched in Alabama,
An old Vietnamese woman torched alive in a hut,
A blind, one legged, starving Kabul child stepping on a land
mine,
A Detroit three-year-old gunned down by cross-fire while
playing in the front yard,
A small, terrified terrier being used for bait in a dog fight,
A 911 plane passenger, Syria,
Koalas caught in Australian bushfires.

One question which kept hammering at my head , like it
had on hers , was about *the homeless souls, 'when the*
entry doors to that fetid place are closed and locked
forever, what will happen to the still unrepentant, and 'the

morally bankrupt who feel no need for such banalities? and 'the virtuously destitute, dishonorable barbarous wicked beasts, committing the basest of acts to the detriment of all worlds? [The Homeless Souls]

Yes, indeed, where will these people go when the doors to Hell are closed?

Ah, this is so uncanny, but I have also often yearned to do exactly the same things that this versatile poet has wished to do in The Ma'am in the moon,

May I romp on for all time, floating joyfully from peak to peak,
exploring the nethermost depths of each crater,
polishing rocks as I go.
My smile paramount to the light given off by this celestial orb of night,
 to be seen by the children of all places,
for these are the souls that must be inspired.

....
And call to mom, call to dad, come and look, come and see,
the beautiful lady on the beautiful blood red moon tonight.
What mind- bowing imagery! It revived the comatose romantic in me, redoubling my craving to be that lady in the moon, trying to heal a topsy -turvy world, where war is glorified, lynching is normalized, peace icons are demonized , and children are killed just like that !

Before signing off, let me confess, that this poet, has inadvertently turned me into an insomniac, because I have found myself returning to the soothing cadences of these poems, not only during the day but also during nights, and enjoyed every moment of this literary gem, which I found beautifully introspective, and profoundly philosophical coupled with a unique lyrical resonance.

Lending my voice to her voice, I have also hoped with her, for a better world. If peace and love have to reign in this world, it should be NOW!

Hands extended in amity,
words spoken with utmost sincerity,
atonements completed and conscience wiped clean.
If ever a time requires making music, it should be now.

Feeling the mirth and gaiety of the wind in our hair,
hastening without fear of doom, toward an ecstasy both spiritual and absolute.
If ever we desire to jump and shout for the joy of living, it should be now,
Loudly celebrating with body, mind, heart, soul. Let it start here, [Escalation]

May all of us, take a leaf from the poet, become a bird and sing *in deep- throated tones,* enjoying the *zoom, the sweep, and the rush of a soft landing after a rough flight.* [*The Flight*], throw away the useless twigs of grouses and grudges,
keep only the uplifting ones for building a nest of memories.

I'll recall, when my final dawn sneaks forward, the many grades and pitfalls I stumbled through while remaining upright. I'll keep walking in shades of beauty, seeing the twinkling stars play,

To me, this book appeared like a whiff of fragrant air in these bleak times, when the corona virus has brought mankind to its knees. As I read on, I also heard, a new dawn stirring.

All around us, bells are ringing,
heralding the new dawn to come.

And those in crypts,
though they be dead, release the hopeful breath
they have held for so very long and join the gleeful celebration.

[Bells Ringing]

Here is one book which needs to be cherished by every lover of poetry, and to be part of every library. And since the book is about the need to ask questions, let me ask the poet MY question, 'when should we expect your next book?'

Dr. Santosh Bakaya, internationally acclaimed for her poetic biography of Mahatma Gandhi, [Ballad of Bapu, Vitasta , 2015,] is an academician -poet- novelist -Ted Speaker -creative writing mentor, and runs a very popular column *Morning Meanderings* in *Learning and Creativity .Com.*

Her latest books are *Songs of Belligerence* and a biography of Martin Luther King Jr. *Only in the Darkness can you see the Stars.*

Hello Wonderful Readers:

This, being the second edition of "Big Questions, Little Sleep," continues the search for answers to the questions seen below. The questions persist, as they should for all peoples every place on our glorious planet. It's a delightful club, this humanity, and I am so grateful and honored to be a part of it.

Questions for the ages:

How will we ever reconcile the Robin Hood aspect of time —that time is both the thief of youth and the giver of memories at the same time?

Why does one year slip into another so seamlessly, yet until the year is done, progress seems to be a fleeting thing? It's only in looking back that we see all the accomplishments made.

Why do the dead never report back to us? Is it because somehow we have not connected death properly with time?

Anton Chekhov said, "The role of the artist is to ask questions, not to answer them."

So, as definitive as these poems may appear, they still leave questions or questions on questions.

With Much Gratitude,

Linda, July 2020

Table of Contents

PART ONE-TIME

THEORY:

Pusher (3)
The Swiftness of Time (5)
Time as Harlequin (7)
Dream's Garden (8)
Escalation (9)
Time (10)
Atop the Hill (11)
Beautiful Ruin (12)
Fortress As Duet in Latter Days (13)
Winter's Witches (14)
The De-evolution of Bandaids (15)
A Moment In A Cup (16)

SEGMENTS:

Chronology (18)
Moment (19)
The Heart's Camera (20)
This Day (21)
The Cards Spoke (22)
Déjá Vu (23)
Day's End (24)
Digging The Day (25)
The First Week of Shattered Dreams (29)
Year Among the Stars (31)

The Message of Breath (35)
Old Age (36)
Age Times Ten (37)

REMEMBRANCE:

Lovely (40)
The Forgotten Life of Velma Hopkins (41)
Sad Passing Youth (42)
The Old Westerns (43)
Time's Yearning (44)
Her Eyes (45)
Dennys At Midnight (47)
Puppy (48)
The Long Lane (49)
Paper Dolls Left in the Rain (51)
Wings (52)
The Wedding (53)
Michael's Memories (55)
Egghead Knew Best (57)
Eric (58)
A Cup of Tea (59)
Bonham, Texas (60)
The Memory of the Words of Doves (62)
Museum (63)

WHEN:

Pillow (65)
Which? (68)
The New Lords (69)
Futuristic Farm (70)
Footsteps That Have Long Faded (71)

History's Outlaws Revised (72)
Changing Hairstyles (73)
Summer's Stand-In (74)
Summer Vacation Memories '66 (75)
Polaroid (76)
The Ticking of Winter's Clock (77)
Painted Walls (78)
Her Movie Script (79)

Last:

Until (80)

PART TWO-DEATH

CONCEPTS AND CONJECTURES

A Grave Question (83)
In Bare Feet (84)
Covet (85)
Before The Sand Stops (86)
Universal Sorrow (87)
Grave (88)
Night Guard (89)
Traces: A Tanka Poem (90)
Six Feet (91)
Gossips (92)
The Gift of Myrrh (93)
Flight (94)
As Alice Said, I Love the Dead (96)

TRIBUTES:

Hands (98)
If Only (99)
Sailor Man (Elegy for Jerry) (100)
His Life Lived (102)
Such Truth in Tears (104)
Zoe Bonham (John Bonham) (106)
Ocasek (108)
The Stone Man (109)
Freak (For Laurie) (110)
Moving Mountains (112)
Girl (Nancy) (114)
Maestro (Elegy for Wilbur) (115)
Just Come Back (116)
A Bluebird Sadly Flown (A Tribute to a Pop Muse) (117)
Zelda (Robin Williams) (118)
John Gone Twice (120)
Bowie (David) (121)
The Search for Nimoy (Leonard) (122)
Tommy Boy (A Tribute To Petty) (124)
The Man In The Derby Hat (125)
The Unmoored (For Pat and Bill) (126)
Berclair (127)
Inge (Daginne) (130)
Ripples On A Pond (For Daniel) (132)
Jan (133)
Jim (Morrison) (135)
The Wise One (136)
Last Day (137)
Tower of Bones (138)
Bequeathing (139)
Urn (140)

A Message From Mom (142)
Last Summer in Galveston (143)

BECAUSE:

Telephone (145)
Upon the Shore (147)
Declaration (148)
Babies (149)
Man in the Bath (150)
Pinned (151)
Small Detail (152)
Bells Ringing (153)
Final Count (154)
Have You Heard the Butterflies Sing? (155)
Intended King Most Deadly (156)
Tolling (157)
Celebrating A Death (159)
Burying My Cat (160)
Schadenfreude (161)
Taurus Of Man (162)
Dead Clocks (163)

BEYOND:

Homeless Souls (165)
What Once Was Once Was There (166)
Cousin May (168)
Chester (169)
Last Train (170)
Ascension (171)
The Ma'am in the Moon (172)

War is Dead (173)
Wolves in Sheep's Clothing (174)
Spoiled Fruit (175)
Part of Me (176)
The Looking (177)
Long Strange Trip (179)
Bus in Heaven (181)
Poe's Annabel Lee (182)
When I Find You Again (Barefoot Dreams) (183)
The Storyteller Within the Blue Latitudes (184)

SOULS:

Conversation (186)
One Man's Karma (187)
Dead Poets and the Lugubrious Living (189)
Intermission (190)
Tomb (191)

TIME

Concepts and Conjectures

Pusher

"The Doctor" stands
at the corner of the street,
smiling at passersby.

His customer base
grows daily
in frigid winter or hot July.

No one knows how long
he's been here,
nor from where
he originally came.

Nor where he goes
when the day is done,
nor even knows his name.

Some see him as
charming and debonair,
others only see him
present an unctuous air.

He offers his product
to those willing to pay
exorbitant prices
day after day.

Women or men,
kids or teens,
the up-and-coming
or the sad has-beens.

Those in his thrall
will steal to get their fix,
destroy their marriages,
even turn tricks.

Will lie to those
who once trusted them,
will kill or sell out others
using foul stratagem.

His specialty's in great demand,
his merchandise is prime.
No, he doesn't sell them drugs,
what he sells is time.

The Swiftness of Time

The ravaged face,
belies a younger life,
enlivened with friendship,
suitors constant at the door.

Time, time, time,
Slow down.

The memory gaps,
deny 90 years
of happy, energetic activity.
A mind where today
relevant history lays imprisoned.

Time, time, time,
Slow down.

Trapped inside hunched backs,
toothless mouths,
and thin-haired pates,
they long to remind us of what really matters
before time deludes us also.

Time, time, time,
Slow down.

We blame the old for hearing loss,
yet we are the ones who stop listening.
They call to us,
their children and such.
Hasty in our dealings,
our clamorous world
drowns them out.

Time, time, time,
Slow down.

Our chronology is set.
Our own annals to be
recited to indifferent ears
if we do not learn.
Vita Brevis.

Time As Harlequin

Some strange trick of the mind, sleight-of-hand, time's hands?
Idleness or fixed energy? Cards,
quickly shuffled. Hocus-pocus. The fast
card shuffler's hands. Prestidigitation.

Pace, disguised as standard routine,
felt as fast or slow;
thus, we register our accomplishments done

by the ticking of the clock or,
the turning of the world.
Those routine beats of time,
sped up, not standard,

or slowed down.
Our false system of reckoning,
calendars
flap quickly through their phases as if by legerdemain,

wizards of time shift the measuring.
The same degree of hour,
second, or minute altered,

grown longer or shorter by our accursed invitation,
to watch the harlequin perform,
we lose count

of the acquisition and reward
for tasks and projects completed.
Only in retrospect, at the end
does deft trickery stop.

Dream's Garden

Dip beneath the whirring birds.
Accept the shine as polished silver
that scatters the light,
like woven sunbeams.
Remember your purpose.
You have your house to build.
Learn all that you are capable of,
and remember that worm becomes butterfly.

Escalation

If ever a time comes to whisper peace be with you,
it should be now.
Words breezing gently into another's ear.
Eyes full of hope and joy for the promise of a changed world.

If ever a time happens to speak aloud that you are my friend,
it should be now.
Hands extended in amity,
words spoken with utmost sincerity,
atonements completed and conscience wiped clean.

If ever a time requires making music,
it should be now.
Feeling the rhythm, the dance of the universe,
all sounds for all seasons,
sing, strum, beat, slide, blow, chant.

If ever a time should be for walking,
it should be now.
Wandering in a beautiful world,
learning as we go,
strolling past the familiar and unfamiliar.

If ever it comes to pass that we should run,
it should be now.
Feeling the mirth and gaiety of the wind in our hair,
hastening without fear of doom,
toward an ecstasy both spiritual and absolute.

If ever we desire to jump and shout for the joy of living,
it should be now,
Loudly celebrating with body, mind, heart, soul.
Let it start here,
with you.

Time

In the dark of night he crept,
deft and quick,
this Robin Hood.

He must've been
a thief of time,
because I never saw him.
But one day
when I looked in the mirror,
I realized he'd been there many times.
After all these years,
I grasped how much
of my youth he had taken.
The robber of so many of my minutes.

Yet, he left to me a pile of memories,
of faces and conversations.
A pile growing larger each year,
so he does give back to the poor.

Atop the Hill

I see much from my place atop the hill.
Harried mothers squawking,
old men numb with loneliness,
laced lovers convinced of privacy.

There are no windows here to close,
no way to mute.
All things are present to me,
and I long for forgetfulness.

The sky alternately dark, then light,
it makes no difference here.
My eyes catch some movement.
I spend all time the same way.

Seeing footprints in the snow,
seeing sweat dripping from hot bodies.
Each season has its own true stamp.
Watching them all rotate through the years.

Across generations,
I observe similar human actions,
familiar, they seldom change their style,
going about their day's business.

Perhaps someone will come relieve me,
but as centuries pass, I realize
there is still no window, and I'll always hear and see
all from atop the hill.

Beautiful Ruin

Within peeling walls,
where spiders and specters now dwell,
and hold court with the dust,
they alone remain,
as the non-derelict guardians,
and holders of this history.
No more to hold the roof aloft
than time itself,
a roof crushed under the weight
of leaves and detritus,
outside would-be invaders
who threaten to force entry,
and destroy the sanctity
of broken glass and tiles.
This grand deconstruction,
splendid in its disrepair.

Fortress As Duet in Latter Days

Nothing to be heard,
but heartbeats and sighs
we hear,
inside,
each other's heads,
as gentle breeze,
and rhythm.

The cosmic magnificence
of our mutual mantra,
chanted in tandem,
over decades.

Simple plans,
and actions assented,
remedies,
good medicine
accrued,
long forgotten laughter,
and so few regrets.

Thoughts,
recollections,
secrets,
inside
a fortress
only we two,
during so many years,
could engineer.

Winter's Witches

When a woman of some age appears,
magick stirs the air around her aura.
She finds her inner wisdom,
and as the forward movement of time proceeds,
within her,
solitude takes first place,
and tranquility leads the parade.

She grows her soul,
while letting the weeds of excess dry up.
She, passing the torch
of an honorable mind and heart.

Feelings, knowledge, spiritual truths,
all purified and purifying,
living right with a fearless heart.

These graceful agers of our world are praised.
They long have been
the banner bearers of life's truths.

The eyes of a woman of many winters
will reflect all you need to know,
and her sorcery will show you how to love.

The De-evolution of Bandaids

Remember when bandaids came in a tin box
instead of flimsy cardboard?
It's as if the hurts
don't need to be protected as much as they once were.

The glamour and illusion of safety
in childhood is today dispelled,

whiskered chins
and palsied hands
offer no safekeeping,

and the mitigation of unhappiness
is no longer a hope.

The illusion of size to security,
shattered.

Falling is still an option,
but now, it's so much harder to get back up.

A Moment In A Cup

What happens when you lay down
a tea bag after you have dipped it?
Does it change that moment into lovely or beastly?
Like the butterfly effect,
but instead of the weather
something happens within your heart and head?
I think not.
For lovely moments are earned with smiles.
And beastly moments are earned with lies.
So, do and think the waking days of your life
as you would in your most pleasant dreams,
and you will never have to say
you're sorry in either.

Segments

Chronology

Crawling and teetering across vast distances
around objects of gargantuan proportions.

Always running,
through instructive days,
tucked among an illusion
of unending summers,
crafted and carefree.

Progressing across miles of possibilities,
with life open at the far end.

The final glide up,
through the enduring curvature of time.

Moment

That frozen moment in time,
forever etched in memory,
what life remains,
experienced in stops and starts,
starts always back to that moment.
Regret revisited,
constantly.
Another chance, another chance,
that's all you need
to turn the tide,
float you back to shore.
Feet safely on the shore,
sand on your feet,
to tell you you're back.
If only you could go back,
to right before
that forever etched moment in time.

The Heart's Camera

That second of time caught in an eyepiece,
as the camera's shutter loudly snapped.
The capturing of blissful calm and ease
on young faces of those photographed.

This image will stand as a testament
to the history of good friends well met,
to whom, to what, and to how it was then,
photostat narrative of this quartet.

Stout hearts worn on their sleeves that noon,
sleeves now faded with the passing of time.
And so this photo keeps fading too,
as each one arrives at the finish line.

This Day

This day,
my best friend and I met for the first time.
We two Taureans,
born on a common month and day,
also sharing a stubborn nature.

This day,
secrets are told and laughter ensues,
always so glad to see each other.
She's a good listener,
has never met a stranger,
there's never dread toward our time together.

This day,
when they ask me about quirks,
I can tell them with ease,
fussy about getting nails done,
grapes and spaghetti are taboo,
cheese and vanilla ice cream are personal favorites.
She doesn't like swimming.
Doctors visits are a breeze.

This day,
Watching TV together,
I glance at her.
People often comment on her beautiful face,
and I tell them I know.
Her eyes and ears always so attentive to others,
I see why they have fallen in love.

That day,
At almost 17, she died.
I held her dog collar in my hands.
Enduring love for her still kisses my heart.

The Cards Spoke

On the day no one was looking,
everyone aged,
only by a day,
but that day went fast,
as the cards were shuffled so quickly.
It was as if
a parlor trick was being presented.
And people wept, knowing
the chance to slow down time
had eluded them.
The clock's hands would spin.
When no one was listening,
life spoke secrets
for earning immortality,
long lost knowledge was confessed.
and all were deemed unlucky.
The flip of the cards
was so loud that they drowned out
any chance to catch the words.
And people wept, knowing
that to live forever
had eluded them.
That last day would come.

Déjà Vu

The sensation of returning,
to a place you've never been,
runs cold in your veins.
What clues still lie in wait
to help remind you
of when you had been here,
and what you had done while?
Such a common, human experience,
unexplained.
A slippage of the mind?
Or in the fabric of the cosmos?
Too prevalent to be coincidence,
but its purpose still left unfolded.
A call back or forward?
If so, to where we do not know,
for now.

Days End

What spurs us when darkness descends,
to repeat the same ablutions and rituals night after night?
Superstitious fear of breaking a cosmic chain,
or a laziness we require to undo the stresses of the day?
Or maybe just comfort,
to know we're at home where security lies.

A Cuban Bruja
in purple robes,
lights candles, recites invocations.
Honorable Magick
conjured for purposes only she knows.

Lovers in embrace,
sex the focus,
staving off not only desire, loss of energy.
The aim is nightly exhaustion
in the hopes of peaceful, dreamless sleep for both.

A tottering old woman
feeds her beloved cats,
tucks them into soft cat beds,
pets them in the hopes
they will accept her affection and treat her with same.

A young Asian woman,
Tai Chi for relaxation,
incense burnt.
Soothe the body, soothe the soul,
these nocturnal mechanizations.

Night may simply be meant to bring peace,
however we seek it,
hopeful discovery of serenity at day's end.

Digging The Day

In the early bright of this damned yet blessed universe,
the sweet taste of white madness numbs my tongue,
and cigarette smoke inhaled fills my lungs.

At the foot of the bed, that chick's panties lay over my feet,
sheets are leaking off the bed all over the floor.
It goes that way, doesn't it?
We slept with an open window, now feeling winter's bite,
but before that, we rode the carousel of snow covered
horses.
Horses with sharp shoulders which poked us here and there,
rode up and down, around and around.
The ride went on for hours, I prayed it would last all night
long.
My tobacco stained fingers dipping into that holy grail.
Later, we dosed each other with buzz and each named a
deity,
not that flash in the pan spiritual high,
I mean the long essence of Buddha,
rapturous, organic.
She, an ebon angel who cracked my spine, my secrets.
She absorbed my immortality and she will share it for
generations on end.
That midnight blue chick I met last night on MacDougal.
Her demeanor upbeat and her sensibilities more
conventional than Benny's,

whom I, by queer chance, met six days ago,
He, with the moniker I assigned him.
He with his pocketful of bennies, I enjoyed them both
for a few turns of the earth.

At the meridian hour, she and I hiked down to the corner
market for more smokes.
She saw someone she dug across the store
and I only saw her back as my last view,
and so plays the waltz.
But, I'll be honest,
competing for her company was not in the cards.
I'm a lover, not a fighter,
a libertine.
I only wish to uncover the truth of lovers: I want, I wish, I
hope, I love,
such deep-seated thoughts inside the simplicity of those
words,
Empty suffering.

Lucien, Lucien where art thou?
You who taught me modern thought and vision,
to be au courant if you will.

As afternoon shifts forward,
I find my way down the road to where the coffee shop
and the brothel sit as neighbors.
It's time to stretch my social latitudes,
and so I tell that young cat whose name keeps eluding me,

as we walk back to my pad;
I use drugs to grow the earth,
derange my upbringing, and not make life seem so dull.
Boredom is so dangerous for the mind and the veins.

On the walls, shotgun prints explode with color,
I tell him I'm new around here,
my voice once spoke from the West,
My fingerprints are on display back there where the cubes
locked us up,
The parks in San Francisco aren't what they used to be!
We both laugh.
Later, I tell him more.
My words are my bonds which I choose to unleash at times,
He un-cuffs my wrists so I may use my hands expressively
to pursue an artisan bent that represents me now in this
time, in this place,
and later he wanders out the door.

When the soft diffused dim begins,
I start to hear men, women, and children
in the building weeping.
I wish to weep myself as I gaze out the window
into the darkening sky,
and see the lid to the vault of heaven
thrown open and diamonds spilling out.
They remind me of those spilled sheets and the sexual
ambience of my space.

Living alone without talk is how I feel my peace.
However, that moon in my head
is now again speaking to me, loud and with great truth.
As the twelfth hour tips over,
I decide I'm gonna fall in with some other beats
who can dig the smell of life.
I know just where to go, and I hear the drum beat and
poems within as I approach.
My solitary walk home in the early morning along smoky
streets, obscuring people and cars,
brings back memories of the fogs in Frisco.
Tears and loneliness and death,
it ends that way for everybody, doesn't it?

The First Week of Shattered Dreams

This lone week plays as a century long,
with each new normal nothing more
than a ridiculous display,
aberrant.
A pretentious pageant with no real import.
To comport myself by common standards
while I stand at a crossroads ,
every juncture leading to furthering
the weight of my bereavement,
indecision, at this time, the only reality for me.

Your intentions are seemingly admirable,
but logic is not useful to a broken heart,
one ruptured by loneliness,
a body disabled with grief,
as I try to stand on legs
that feel as if they belong to a lesser creature,
one without cartilage or bone.

The only lightening that I sense
is a part of my soul torn from me,
given freely by me and allotted to him,
so that I may, in some way, go with him
and he would not be alone.

So when you, here in my space, seek to distract me
to have me believe in a happier world,
your voice, meant to soothe, only serves as an irritant,
as do all living things at this time.
Even the rising sun preceding the fair weather
arrives as a mocking burlesque.
I can almost hear the mirth
from every budding tree and woody shrub.

Leave me now,
to my own imaginary universe,
replete with memories of my choosing,
and the belief that
he still breathes in the other room.
This deception will be my salvation
for future weekly centenaries.

Year Among the Stars

April: Leo the lion
Most prominent constellation in this night sky,
And in like a lion
Comes Regulus Alexander,
All 7 1/2 pounds of him,
Wailing,
A glorious sound,
His grandparents buy him a star,
His namesake,
But to Rita and Alan
He will be known as Rex.

May: Virgo the Maiden
Marked,
Up there,
Rex's teenage aunt
Holds this 1 month wonder.
He holds her finger
With strong grasp,
She doesn't want to let go either.

June: Libra and her Scales
Noticeable in the night sky,
Rex, 2 months
Has gained some weight,
People's comments,
Beautiful, healthy,
A toothless, social smile
Makes others do the same.

July: Scorpius the Scorpion
Easily seen,
One day shy of 3 months,
In this time of the stinging predator,
Rex feels the sting of the needle
For the third time in his life.
Necessary inoculations,
Beautiful, healthy.

August: Sagittarius the Archer
Extrusive in the deep dark,
Rex, adventuresome,
His 4-month old chin
Covered with puréed peas,
A mouth full of watery cereal
He grins, drools,
He points much as the archer does.

September: Capricorn the Goat
Stands out,
Rex, 5 months in,
A discovery of toes.
Rita worries what else
Might get tasted
As time goes by.

October: Aquarius the Water Bearer
Splendid and bright,
6 months of baths
Still haven't curbed
The desire to splash.
To Rex, it's funny
Slamming down
Small bath toys into the water.

November: Pisces the Fish
Obvious,
7 months,
Rex discovers more
Of what his body can do.
Arms and legs,
Flailing,
Simultaneously one way and the other.

December: Aries the Ram
Unmistakable above,
8 months,
Tis' the season to be jolly.
Rex is this,
Barring diaper and clothing changes,
But Santa will still come
For this willful, little person.

January: Taurus the Bull
Such brilliance in this crisp weather,
9 months of yes, yes,
Now frequently no, no,
Becoming more stubborn,
He further explores,
Crawls,
To where he should not go.

February: Gemini the Twins
Striking,
10 months,
Routine checkup,
Silly Rex repeating silly things
To get attention.
He draws two-year-old twins into his world.
Two unvaccinated.

March: Cancer the Crab
Clear at night,
There it is,
Measles,
Horrible morbilli,
11 months of great health,
Then he suffers greatly,
Prolonged symptoms.
After,
Further diagnosis,
Encephalitis.

April: Leo: Revisited
His parents
Have done all they can
To save him.
For this family,
The Vedic man
Spine and heart affected.
And when one night,
He who comes
And ultimately guides us all,
Picks him up in his arms,
Places him inside his star.
Rex does not burn,
Just continues to sleep.
On Earth,
Gentle April showers
Follow him into the ground.

May-May (eternal): Regulus Alexander
Brightest, most twinkling
In the night sky.

The Message of Breath

That first breath announced,
with a cacophony of wailing.
In youth,
a pretty girl passes by,
takes his breath away,
albeit for short time.
Suffering twilight years,
out of breath with growing frequency,
distances walked lengthen with age.
The top of the staircase
might as well be Mount Olympus.
Then the last breath,
the death rattle always so unexpected,
in spite of its inevitability.

Breathing defines us as living,
Exercise, sensualness, anxiety quickens breath,
sleep or spiritual harmony deepens it.

This is our message,
sent out into the world.
We are here, we are here.

Old Age

It came, and we met it head on.
We stepped into the midnight taxi
and never flailing,
never failing,
we never forgot to love,
and to live with utmost purpose.

We had thick skin,
and were thick with memories.

Nature's taxi,
also yellow with age,
delivered us
to the place we had earned.

Face to face with old age,
it came, and we met it head on.

Age Times Ten

Age 8

She said she loved his shirt,
so he wore it every day.

Age 16

He said he loved her hair,
then, she styled it always the same.

Age 24

She checked the taste of his coffee in the morning
and always gave him the pizza slice with the most
pepperoni.

Age 30

He built her a library room because she loved to read.
While he stood dusty and sweaty from the construction,
she told him he was better looking than Clooney.

Age 50

At her first poetry reading, she caught movement in the
audience
as he sat in the audience smiling and waving and
he had the loudest applause.

Age 70

She helped him button his shirt,
although she had arthritis, too.

Age 80
Side by side, they lie and dream together
beneath the grassy green and starry nights.

Remembrance

Lovely

Lovely was born,
Mid 19th,
as Harpers Ferry led the news.
She lived from telegraphs to telephones,
trains to planes.
Long enough to like Ike twice.

Her tolerance was like a ruler
balanced on an index finger.
In middle-age, a rigid center,
in youth and old age
pliable at both ends.

An incredible metamorphosis of man,
about a century long,
viewed through her eyes.
Who could not be curious,
who could not continue to wonder
with all the fascinations already seen?
A happy life filled with thrills,
always a new this, a new that.

A wonderful life,
full of both short, fulfilling contentments,
and numerous joyously anticipated adventures,
She remained honest in her dealings with others,
A contributing factor to her long life,
her final thoughts were private,
but the smile on her face told the tale.

Lovely in life,
Lovely in death,
She is
Lovely.

The Forgotten Life of Velma Hopkins

From room to room,
she wanders and examines,
each room set with half drawn shades.

So many things leave no impression,
but there are pictures here and there,
that briefly incite a quicker heartbeat
and some pattering of the tiny feet of remembrances.

A vague memory,
almost a seed taking root,

If she could have recalled:

He was always a plane taking off
against the wind,
the smell of Aqua Velva in his cheek.

But, these, only mere images,
fleet and fading.

And if it hurts to remember
once being happy,
then she feels no pain.

Sad Passing Youth

The best of friends, all so close,
Six different cities sent these sons and daughters
to this place, at this time,
to the Nexus, the axis, the center,
where hearts met and became glad,
concordance almost spiritual,
differing talents, dreams and hopes, but many the same.

We had each other's backs,
took meals together with no worries of tomorrow,
or that we might ever part for the last time.
For then it was enough for the moment to share bread,
to listen to each other's tales,
learn of each other's lives,
to speak of the world and its meaning, for us, then.

Although summers were spent apart,
with letters flying back-and-forth,
the autumn brought a reunion of mirrored hearts and minds.
Open-minded, fearless youth;
you taunted us,
and pulled us into a safe cocoon, assuring lasting calm.
We, as those before us and those to follow,
fell prey to your temporary charms.

How we resent, yet long for you at the same time,
You are not the peaceable condition you professed to be
at that long ago time.
None will be wiser than we,
Not until they are as we are now,
but let them enjoy, and revel, today,
for sadly, passing youth is all too brief.

The Old Westerns

No more heroes on horses named Trigger,
No more rugged, chapped, white hatted figures.
The bad guys today do not always wear masks,
At least not the exact kind they did in the past.

Though crime existed in those olden days,
In the end, the wicked were locked away.
Paladins were not treated with such disdain,
Nor with such peoples' champion smear campaigns.

Robbers rode over steel rails to make swipes,
Hijackers now fly steel birds and take lives.
Highwaymen robbed folks along dry dusty trails,
Ponzi takes fortunes through electronic mail.

Robber barons dishonestly stole wealth,
Computer hackers do the same through stealth.
Telegraphs allowed graft across the flat land,
Now accomplished today with mobile broadband.

Desert gangs of thieves hid gold in dark caves,
Turbaned hordes cross hot deserts to enslave.
Guns were drawn behind bat wing doors of saloons,
Guns drawn inside hallways of our children's schools.

Are we safer today? Sheltered from crime?
Truly living in a more civil time?
So, make fun of Roy and the Lone Ranger, too,
But heroes are fewer and that's much to rue.

Time's Yearning

I stood across the street,
from the place where I'd lived,
from infancy to university,
oh, what I wouldn't give,

to reverse time and see my friends again,
to whom I was so close.
I summon sunny days and then replay,
those I love most.

I lost my dog last year,
and never was she found,
return to then and have her reappear,
result rewound.

But I must make do with how I live now,
let when and where be right.
Eschew good memory to me endowed,
so I can sleep at night.

Her Eyes

Her eyes saw slow descent,
the lagging of thoughts
as old age unravels the last threads of youth.
The trick of slow time,
secreting the true clock,
a jarring unveiling.

Her eyes saw new life,
so lovely and pure.
Rich in inspiration to be the harbinger
of tranquility,
contentment looking toward,
safe future unfolding.

Her eyes saw beauty,
breathtaking vistas.
True nature simple and complex juxtaposed,
hypnotic with its strength,
drawing the eye above,
sideways, and below.

Her eyes saw desperation,
betrayal's sad price.
A once mirthful person now left humorless,
never again to trust,
because pain
is not worth such cost.

Her eyes saw marked improvement,
grand achievement.
New inventions and an uplifting of mankind
fueled by rare mix,
compassion wed to ambition,
selfless and earnest.

Her eyes saw new lands.
White sands along blue seas,
translating accord into rapport.
New foods, music, friends,
new countries harboring
the promise of peace.

Her eyes saw merciful death.
The dark weight of disease
held earthbound by gravity, ceding to the lightness
of a soul now uncaged,
an unholy alliance
of germs and flesh unlinked.

Her eyes saw the story of life,
a tale worth being told.
Who else will be tasked with making certain life goes on?
So that others may know
the ken of each breath,
so that others may truly see.

Dennys At Midnight

It seems now so long ago.

Hashing out problems,
and firming up philosophies
over priced right coffee and pancakes until 2:00 a.m.

Learning the art of conversation
from my tribe-
Long ago,

They still walk beside me.
I hear their voices ring and sing
in my memories.

Comfortable silences and smiles
or raucous conversation
disclosing mutual experiences.

Friends gathering in that nocturnal eatery,
lending support,
walking in while others walked out.

Today, I am alone in my thinking.

How I miss one of
America's best therapy lounges.

How I long for the glue of firm friends
that kept me from falling apart.

How I long.

Puppy

Puppy showed up on the day I was born.
Soft brown fur and marbles in his right paw
along with button eyes. He showed his age
like me over time. Fur thinning as with mange,
with tears in the fabric as if one gnawed
away that fur to leave a threadbare body torn.

He's ever been to me a source of comfort.
Stuffing, leaking out, making his body flatter,
buttons loosed, holes sewn shut serve to protect
from viewing brutal acts we say that matter.
Race hate and death of innocents to correct,
as Father, Son, and Holy Ghost assert.

The clack of gewgaws stay as a plea for my prayers:
Hear me, my childhood way to summon the ears
of the holy ones taught to me,
fabric splits leak blood, sweat, tears of many years
are now sewn shut. Broken heart healed. The key
to lessening my pain. Each wound and nick
repaired with care.

His unselfish act reflects
ravages of time and the human soul.
He's helped me keep my idealism.
A lifelong companion to be extolled,
unseemly enough to cause a schism,
yet grant no pathos, there's been no neglect.

The Long Lane

As a child walking the long lane,
I met a furry pal.
When we parted at the fork,
he licked my face and disappeared.
My face stayed wet.
These were my first tears.

As a teen walking the long lane,
I met an old woman.
When we parted as friends,
she hugged me goodbye and left.
I felt something missing.
This was my next loneliness.

As a young woman walking the long lane,
I met a young man.
When we reached the fork,
he was the one whom I could not let go.
My heart stayed aflutter.
This was my first love.

At some point while walking the long lane,
This man whom I had wed,
went from young to old and frail.
We parted at the fork in the road of life.
He looked into my eyes and then beyond the trees.
My chest got tight.
This was my worst grief.

Now I alone am walking the long lane,
For the Lane is my home.
When I reach the fork,
I will choose neither path but sit and stay.
For what I have not yet seen, felt, nor heard
must not exist.
This is the place I belong.

Paper Dolls Left in the Rain

I must remember to grab the right half of truth,
that clarity sometimes breathed at dawn.
And remember the radiant substance
of our friendship.

Knowing you long ago,
and all the colorless girls and boys,
and what transpired
within a mere fraction of my life,
might seem to others as weak,

but what power it held.

Hearing of your silent death
throws such wistfulness my way,
and I can no longer truly feel
our reminiscences without you at the other end.

And though I wish to stop
and really relive my best years,
the ritual of time is pulling me along,
pulling me beyond
the demarcation line
between childhood to adult.

Wings

As the beating of the wings of birds,
my mother's fluttering eyelashes
seen with my infant eyes,
as I studied the face of the first person I ever loved.

As the beating of the wings of birds,
my friends' fluttering hands
emphatic with anger, comic with hilarity, revelatory with gossip,
as I listened to both their wisdom and their folly.

As the beating of the wings of birds,
the fluttering in my chest,
the first time I saw him, the first time he touched me
and all times thereafter.

As the beating of the wings of birds,
the soft fluttering of ancient wings,
the wings of those who come to comfort me,
sit at my bedside
sharing with me my final hours.

The Wedding

Along an alabaster shore,
with purposeful steps,
walks a man
toward a tiny, steepled structure.
Much to his delight,
it's his wedding day,
until cruel fate intercedes.
Passing beneath the tree,
rendered unconscious by a falling branch,
he sleeps as if the sleep of Morpheus
for a time.
Upon awakening,
he has forgotten.
He leaves the island,
lives a life elsewhere.
In doddering old age,
most memories have faded,
for this recent widower,
but something sparks a recollection
of that little church.
He knows he must return.
He walks in.
There, a newly widowed woman sits
as she has for one hour every day,
beginning at the exact minute of the nuptials
which never took place
60 years ago.

Their tears reflect all the words
unspoken between them,
during these many years gone by.
When the priest arrives a few minutes later,
they stand, and take up
where they should have six decades before.
It's a happy day.

Michael's Memories

Michael's at the locked door
staring in the window beyond the glass,
waiting for the owner's key to turn
and bring him a smile of pages,
as he recalls the old bookstores of his youthful days.
The glare of fluorescents reflecting off
the lily whiteness of paper,
the touch of supple leather and the smell of binding glue.
The weight of multiple tomes upon his arms,
muscular in their day.
The once muscular arms of Michael.

Michael's on the mountain's high top
watching flexible branches sway.
Shadows play around him
reminding of times around the campfires,
with friends telling genial and generous stories,
wearing vests for warmth as midnight draws near
and upon still burning coals lie
the vestiges of burned hot dogs
and dripping marshmallows.
The smell of coffee grounds and pine in his nose,
pine tree scent in his nose.
The once juvenile nose of Michael.

Micheal's holding his guitar
and strumming up and down the fretboard.
Waiting for his fingers to imitate
the ease of moving the strings.
Remembering the first-rate songs of his yesterdays.
Familiar chords constructing glorious harmonies
massaging the ears.
Musical satisfaction by means of limber digits,
nature's physical gift once sent to his hands.
beauty produced by him,
from the once bending fingers of Michael.

Egghead Knew Best

An elderly Great Aunt and I once
played a game of Trivial Pursuit
with my youngest brother
and his friends.
At one point,
some kid asked my dad for an egg
to stiffen up his Mohawk hair style.
My Aunt then asked him
if he always played his records backwards.
The kid replied that it wasn't necessary,
because all today's demons
instead played CD's.

Eric

In High School
we were friends.
In college, one of
three roommates
for six months.
One of my favorite
New Years's Eve celebrations
was spent with him until
the early morning hours.
right before midnight.
We went to a brightly lit
liquor store and bought two pints of
vodka for fifty cents a bottle,
one peppermint, the second grape.
He dropped out and
went to hairdresser school
where he styled wigs
that then set atop styrofoam heads
and I would drive him to the school
with his 'homework',
windows of the car rolled up
against the blasting Texas winds,
bouffants in place.
Later, he went to law school,
and I wonder
if he only takes cases
that involve suing people
who give bad haircuts.

A Cup of Tea

I am in need of a sip of her tea,
from a cup that burns my fingertips,
rolls onto my tongue past quiet lips.
My ears willing to hear history,
old stories born from my family tree.
A resurrection of those folks long dead,
becoming animated in my head,
the songs of my fathers', sweet melody.

She has a way of telling those old tales,
breathing life into personalities,
keeping tea and family lore flowing.
For me not to listen would be betrayal
of her and my ancestors' memories.
So my love for tea and family keeps growing.

Bonham, Texas

Springs's leaves fall limp and wet
and hug the gentle bough
from showers that quench the land.
Flowers of pansy and hyacinth
blossom beside the long porch,
and upon the meadow's splendor,
we stand awed against waves of bluebonnets.

Within the shimmer of summer,
the farm is an active place.
During a long walk uphill,
we wend paths active with animal life and birds
and quickly flowing streams,
or stroll across green pastures
in need of mowing
as grasses tickle our ankles.
We avoid 'The Bottoms,'
where the tusked wild boar live,
because no entreaty will appease them.
If by chance they should pass by,
we wear our armor on our hips.

In the drier days,
while leaves sleep and dream
of their reincarnation as new buds,
Autumn deeply inhales summer's breath
and exhales that breath as its own.

In winter, the night is so dark
that even prayers are invisible.

There is no light, except from the fire pits
and a small front porch bulb.
In the dusk of day,
the walks seem twice as long,
for now the streams are thick with ice
and the paths lack tracks.
Everything, but us,
sleeps with the leaves,
And although the way seems lengthened,
it gives us time to dream our own dreams.

The Memory of the Words of Doves

Kind words leave no scars.
Instead, they leave caresses on
the memory of the words of doves,
beautiful feathers sent by friends,
soft as a bed of creamy blossoms.

We all remember what happened years ago.
The easy way some people spoke to us,
and kept their oaths.

Yesterdays,
when every dove lent their voices
to the glory of the world,
and tenderness and peace brought beauty.

So, for today, I wish you peace.

Museum

To the casual eye,
a roomful of old, dusty objects,

scrolls of great words
containing broken promises,

the hardest days of time captured,

man's progress built one culture at a time.

And while the present stands full
of promise and difficulty,
the past did send forth wings of hope,
some forgotten, some ignored.

And it's good to embrace
the backstories of so many forgotten nights.

In this sea of iron, stone, wood, and fabric,
it's amazing to see
how beautifully imperfect we are.

When

Pillow

Certain nights upon
sleep's carousel, pillow dreams.
My diary,
tranquil or horrific,
ancestral remembrance,
visitations.
At my pillow's command,
Morpheus draws forth,
slips between the sheets,
and mirrors the pale ones,
regrettable as lost or found,
vestiges of angels or beasts, that my pillow,
in its wisdom, favors to dance before me,
lay bare, pull from its pages
annals of yesterday
when youth sang to me.
Although my tongue
is stilled in hushed sleep,
old memories seep from the fabric
which covers that soft
warm headrest,
reminds me of what I must never forget.

Some nights, slumbers ride
sleep's carousel, pillow dreams.
My weathervane,
the sly statue of time
poses fleetingly while
rest is in progress.
As my pillow insists,
Machiavelli comes,
slips between the sheets, punctures restful
peace with
fanciful images and thoughts,
unrealistic and innately inchoate.
My pillow offers only fabrication,
in its wisdom, as solution
to my current problems.
Today's present
to which I'm exposed,
the now alone matters
and within this lightless, still room
the fluffed down absorbs
the ah-ha
which I'll forget upon awakening.

Some nights, repose mounts
sleep's carousel, pillow dreams.
My oracle,
symbolic messages
spoken as mystic words,
foreshadowing.
At my pillow's urging,
Pythia appears,
slips between the sheets, summons her dark
vapors,
presaging tomorrow's warrant,
patchy fantastic illusions, that my pillow,
in its wisdom, promises to bring to pass.
These smudgy imaginings,
illusions of unborn
realizations
long coveted,
the prophet's kind futures,
fill my head and heart, like the weft
and woof woven into
cushioned pads,
fears for the next day forgotten tonight.

Which?

If you could choose
your future told,
or the answer
to a haunting mystery
from the past revealed,
which of the two
would you choose?

The New Lords

The old gods hover meekly in the sky,
silver helms or tiaras,
hair of gold or ebony,
or rust, snowy, flaxen, that typify all races.
Nobility shaken as apprehension builds,
new images fill ageless eyes on childlike faces.
Mysterious changelings,
catch their rapt attention,
man as woman, old turns young,
and all sorts in between.
Old creations overshadowed
by mortal reinventions.

Futuristic Farm

(A Prose Poem)

A little house on thirty-six acres of refuge, outside a small Texas town, accessible only by one narrow, perilous, rutted dirt road. My father's farm, weekend retreat, brought him back to his small-town upbringing. Reminded him that the actual beauty of the world, woods and streams, "The Bottoms" and birds, could still exist even this close to urban life. A rural, pastoral farm; a house with featherbeds, cots for extra bodies, mowing pastures, riding horses, barbecuing, tire swings and hammocks, homemade ice cream fresh from the churn, happy, slow days and nights. Chasing after bees, a favorite pastime of my brothers, seems always to revert to being chased by bees, a buzzy revenge for a disturbed afternoon nap. Stunning sunsets seen from the porch swing reflecting the promise of meeting the Divine. Halcyon days now coming to an end, the government is buying those acres, as a reservoir is coming. The little house and pasture, even the tree planted in my father's memory after his death, all will soon be submerged. Maybe someday beings from "out there" will explore our planet and find this little piece of Americana, becoming so rare, as similar bucolic scenes fade into obscurity. Their courage took them millions of miles to come here, but first they'll have to brave that narrow, perilous, rutted dirt road.

Footsteps That Have Long Faded

The sounds of quick pace, long marching faded,
specters of those who fought for peace grown pale.
Soldiers' visages evaporated,
keepers and protectors who did not fail.
We, attuned to whispered gait in their wake,
where those who fought the monsters disappeared,
under vast sandy shores beside fruited plains,
bugle's wake-up call dim in their ears.
Brothers in arms, peers with resolute tread,
no more torment beneath the stars above,
our heroic champions now long dead,
unvexed by blast or salvo, life's work done.

Echoes of booted feet going through paces.
we who honor them, still listen for traces.

History's Outlaws Revised

Once upon a time,
the knowers knew,
then devotion to the written word
was squelched.

Once used for remembrance,
there was birthed a forbidden bloom of ink,
and truth, as king, was tumbled from the throne.

The tendency for reflection became lost
as we gave over to the inconsequential,
never more imagining our potential.

It's easier to hold on to today
than to reach for tomorrow.
And with our history lost
in the dark abyss of forgetfulness,
our destiny will be set by others.

And we'll go where we are taken.

And all the songs you,
as an individual, now sing
silently inside the now,
will come to fade.

Without convictions,
we stand as cogs
within the clocks
as time marches forward.

Changing Hair Styles

As the years roll on, don't change hair styles too often.
The hurry of these changes
will give you too many false starts.
Let your coiffure make you steadily individual,
and stay the course.
In life's quick wonderland,
brush and comb
following a necessary format for steadfastness.

Hair as designed tenor,
a dormant symbol of
effort, patience, perseverance.
Therein lies real beauty,
for the fair arranging of plans,
without demanding that
one day must be the same as the next.

Consistently bad hair days: the badge
of disordered dimwits,
of too hasty relocation,
too quick rethinking,
and no comprehensive procedure
make life purposeless.

Summer's Stand-In
(An Etheree Poem)

Caul
on sky;
the changeling
enters our world
and dims what once shone.
Summer switched to Autumn.
The once bright days seem darker
and the wind becomes heavy blown.
This replacement steeps all in shadow.
Fall, as summer's stand-in, brings dusky air.

Summer Vacation Memories '66

Bicycle card spokes fluttering with ticking thumps,
sunny afternoons under sheets as tents,
the click of go-go boots dancing on pavement

the sound of pop music adding depth and cheer,
bleeping from transistor radios

the lilting ice cream truck,
the snap of freshly laundered damp sheets on clotheslines,
in the summer breeze

the rumbly engine of the bookmobile,
saving us from ennui,
telling tales in books we read,
transporting us to new worlds,
when we get bored
with the same old street

the doppler of cars passing by
as we whiz around on roller skates

porch lights lighting up,
telling us the day is done
and the tired trudge home must begin.

Polaroid

My black and whites,
covered with the chemical smell of fixer,
small images developed onto small paper,
reflecting some most important
moments of my life.

Eighth grade friends,
filmed in school hallways,
or in front of their houses
in pairs, groups, or singly.
High School friends
in the same configuration,
so dear to me, yet lost in time
except on photographic paper.

My younger brother as an infant,
proof he was once so tiny.
Jim Morrison on stage,
his image no bigger than my thumbnail,
yet my proof that he ever existed.

My black and whites,
useless to others,
but treasured by me.

The Ticking of Winter's Clock

My mother died in Winter.
my mother far away.

Spring was to rise in only a few weeks.

It was the fourth of March.
Brown grass and leafless trees
were in endless array outside.

I could hear
the ticking of the clock

as I waited
for the phone to ring.

I have my father,
I told myself.

My father died in Winter.
my father far away.

It was the seventh of March
and again, the green was still to come.

And again,
I could hear
the ticking of the clock

as I waited
for the phone to ring.

Then, I was an orphan.

Painted Walls

The first coat of paint in that cozy kitchen
was a soft yellow that reflected the morning sun.
They drank their coffee there and ate their bacon
and eggs together at the table.
Youth and fortuity were on their side,
that beautiful shirking of what should be done,
saved for later.

The second coat in that kitchen
was a shade of coyote brown to hide
little jellied handprints and the scuffing of shoes.
With full adulthood upon them,
they were often steadier and craftier achievers.

The third coat in the kitchen was the hardest to choose.
They sat there for what seemed like an endless time,
trying to decide what color would be most welcoming to
the new owners.
Finally, having decided, they picked up their meager
belongings,
held each other's hand as they closed the front door,
and hoped that their once upon a time home would have
welcoming walls.

Her Movie Script

Beyond the heavy wooden door,
my grandmother rocks in her chair.
Her eyes are glued to the opposite wall
where the movie of her life plays out.
If only she could remember
the names of the actors.

Until

The tiny boat floated on the open sea,
Until it didn't.
The plumed bird soared on the damp air,
Until it didn't.
The blistering fire brightly alit
trees in the forest,
Until it didn't.
The earth gave tremor
under stock-still feet,
Until it didn't.
And you loved me,
Until you didn't.

DEATH

Concepts and Conjectures

A Grave Question

No answer given,
To query repeated.
To hear just one response,
Would make me believe
The dead exist.

Instead,
Silence weighs,
Dead sound,
But not the dead's response.
They do not exist.

In Bare Feet

Your fondest wish to purge yourself
of all earthly things,
to finally become untethered while in death,
you wished for no grave.
For to puncture Mother Earth
on your behalf,
seemed like such a travesty.

You asked them once
to do this one thing.
To see you into the ground
no longer bound.
No linen wraps to encase,
no heavy markers to keep you in place.

They heard you, smiled,
and nodded their heads.

Their compromise, they felt, would serve you well.

They buried you in bare feet.

Covet

They are selfish and they covet that which
is beyond their reach within their own world
of desire: fellowship-heartfelt,
and sought after.

It has long been their fervent wish, this strong
need that has never come to pass. To hear
what those now estranged have to say,
and to make themselves understood.

They do not communicate
and share their equal visions:
Not among their own kind nor each group with
the other side, still and tacit,
both large crowds remain, each in great fear of
what surrounds, living flesh,
or ghosts that haunt dreams
planning a desperate grab.

For the living and the dead compete,
but should they concur? There will come a time,
if each bloc wishes to survive,
an unchained meeting of the minds, detente
must take place and all competition must end.

Until then each is enslaved by the other.

Before the Sand Stops

Before the sand stops,
and the indrawn of life's breath
is no longer heard.
Before the cessation of thought,
and the stiffening in the cold.
Before the eyes' slow roll back,
and the final, keen fail of the organs,
in the bitter winter of his life,
within this expected altering of circumstances,
the wasted, wizened man,
with the bony and angular face,
prays for a loophole from death.
But there is none,
not even a painless one.

The swim to the farthest pool cannot be changed,
good health is now estranged.
No want of peace can be arranged.
This man, thin as a rail,
with skin that appears as wrinkled garments,
bears the ravages,
endures the vented lingering within the oxygen tent.
And inside the hourglass,
each grain is pulled toward the hungry base,
and like the last tick of a clock,
the sand will stop.

Universal Sorrow

Loss,
such a small word,
but conveying the greatest sense of heartache.
Who among us
has not had the experience
of huge pain
at the loss of a person, place, or thing?
Traumatic, tragic,
in some regards senseless.
Some get through it with effort,
find recovery.
Some never will.

It is the universal sorrow.
Loss,
the one thing affecting all living creatures
other than death
And even death is that.

Grave

There's something wrong with your grave.
There's not the wrong kind of grass covering you,
Nor an incorrect variety of flowers growing atop.
The tombstone looks fine:
The symbols etched into the granite
are perfectly formed,
The dates are right,
Your name is spelled accurately,
The shady tree above is grandly leafed
and suits its purpose.
Yet, there is something wrong.
This grave is wrong
for the simple reason
that you don't belong there.

Night Guard

He walks between,
each grave unseen.
Guards each during,
all the many hours of sunlight.

As daylight fades,
They are afraid.
All those decayed,
Lying deep under deepening night.

He just wants to,
Help them get through,
Nighttime dark hued,
Where there is a lack of candle bright.

To ease their fears,
He spends his years,
Within frontiers,
Of the stony etched headstones bleached white.

Traces

(A Tanka Poem)

Upon my sweet death,
bury me without a box.
Absorbed by kind worms,
my last traces transported
lovingly to fair gardens.

Six Feet

Even the larger than life
get no more than six feet down

at the end.

There's no volcanic snoring
from the sleepers here reposed.
No fanatic cackling from those
who once lived within
now powdery sanatoriums.
Jawbones no longer festive
or with coy wag,
no gummy promiscuity
among once social butterflies.

There's no loathsome musings,
nor clandestine plots against
those who stand above in trodden woe.

There's just common rebellion
against being disturbed.
They wish only to remain unperturbed,
memories obliterated,
no troublesome stockpile
of who had what or who was most superb.

Gossips

Both inside and outside a haunted house
the dead fear you more.
So, avoid them in dark alleys
So that that you do not startle them.
For, I guarantee that they are there.
They like to wander because
they are as curious as cats.
They do enjoy a good look inside windows,
especially of places where they once lived.
Would you deny them the pleasure of remembering
their past?

They only want to live up to their eulogies
of having connected,
and the questions of life never cease,
even for them.

They watch closely
to see and hear what goes on around them,
for there are very few spirits without a face,
and none without ears.

They share news of what they have seen and heard.
I have been told they are some of the most
consummate gossips on the planet.

For this reason, beware of seances,
where the dearly departed might tell all your secrets.
It might make for a most embarrassing night!

The Gift of Myrrh

Veiling the spicy scent of necrosis
that accompanies all bitter death,
using the sweet balm of myrrh,
always a prefigurement to eternal rest.

While the bent forms of priests,
with drab discs for eyes,
collect dropped alms,
and pray by way of bewitching hymns,
as perfumed beasts guard the walls,

the dead will find
an absence of air, but no lack of charity
within their enclosed closets
of silence and isolation.

They will also find no absence of myrrh.

Flight

I think of myself
as a bird with twigs to save,
for a nest of memories,
for remembrance of labors well done,
and much sweet music played.

I have, at times, been queen of all music,
enjoyed the zoom, the sweep , and the rush
of a soft landing after a rough flight.
I never found time for mocking the fates
at the fading view of day,
but made time instead
for singing life in deep-throated tones.

With dearest friends, there was never an end
to what we could talk about and learn,
no terminus to listing ways
in which we could leave the world a better place.
So we stayed patient and waited.
We marveled at how quickly time had elapsed
since the last sunset rolled along.
We hypothesized what might erase all our worlds,
and prognosticated when peace would come again.

I'll recall,
when my final dawn sneaks forward,
the many grades and pitfalls
I stumbled through while remaining upright.
I'll keep walking in shades of beauty,
seeing the twinkling stars play,
fold my frail wings in supplication,

and never cease to pray.
I'll survive the stormy blasts
to walk beneath the archway of a rainbow,
delighting that I did not fail.
And get there just in time to the wind-kissed sea,
then fly lightly on my way,
as the dim of my eyes arrives.

As Alice Said, I Love the Dead

Do you believe we respect the dead
more than the living? We assume their
vision is long and wide.
They don't argue or tell tales out of school,
making it easy to create our own history.
We believe they are free of all ill embrace,
and are of an exclusive club to which we'll want to
be a member. They watch over
us, never asking for the benefit
of anything. Perhaps we believe they will
revisit us-somehow. That being the case,
we would wish for them to knock first!
Perhaps we wonder how the man upstairs
feels about the kind of neighbors we were
to those who now live on His street. At any
rate, better to be safe than sorry.

Tribute

Hands

Hands,
fingers thin like paper,
on this mortal shell.
No evidence these hands
ever held a flower,
played an instrument,
typed a letter,
were ever extended to another to help or heal.

No, these fingertips,
flat and tapered,
stiff,
as it being held rigid against the will
of to whom they belong.

Of all the visible parts of that figure
in the funeral box,
the hands,
the most unnatural and
least human feature left
to share with those who've come to say goodbye.

Whoever can one day correct
this artless feature
will have his name lauded throughout the world.
Because those who view the deceased
see only quiet repose,
except for the hands,
the most glaring testament to death's finality.

If Only

As Tantalus pleaded,
all only ever out of reach,
so shall I,
for the alchemy of properly positioned syllables,
the perfect mathematical equation of sounds,
whispered out from a broken heart,
that allows me to have
that one last minute again
before you take your last breath.

As Garbo bid,
from well lit corners of her stage,
so shall I,
to get that perfect retake,
the best possible script written,
delivered in most dramatic fashion
to re-create the final scene,
to assuage my grief
at the stunning irreversibility
of your death.

Sailor Man (Elegy For Jerry)

Sailor man,
Sailor man,
where did you go?

The memory of you,
written inside that blazing fireball,
sinking below the ever-changing horizon
on a warm Summers eve.

The memory of you,
fluttering among multicolored Autumn leaves,
anymore, fallen,
crisp,
beautiful.

The memory of you,
felt as Winter's chill,
freezing air
breathed into stinging lungs,
winter's chill,
covering an icy landscape
with miles of pristine snow,
untrod.

The memory of you,
heard within the rise and fall
of soft Spring songs,
as the Hymns of birds
heralding new life to come.

Wherever you now bide,
know you are missed,
that you gave great joy and comfort,
to all those adrift,
all at sea.
Sailor man,
you,
who guided us in friendship,
be guided now by the greater hand.
Sail past that ever-changing horizon,
and into glory.

His Life Lived

It's always been bizarre, to me,
how summer's keen glow and blooming
plants continue after a death.
But the dead do speak, reminding
us that our status must remain,
even as the world seems to tilt.

All people in time are messaged,
I hear his laugh on the new wind,
born from hidden depths of the sea.
Although I cannot ken his words,
his voice is as music of dawn,
the melody will ever stay.

The wisest among us say not
to fear what you can face straight on.
The penitent sing never fear
that which speaks to you from your heart.
But dignity of grief, restless,
makes us forget the rules of life.

Always, I'll not give audience
to claimants announcing themselves
as witnesses to secret sin,
betrayers and corrupters need
not march in this somber parade.
Let their dead words drop from dead air.

That door once used to seek you out,
to be glad in your company,
will one day appear to me.
I'll hear the gentle knock of love,
know who stands on the other side,
and I'll know I want to answer.

Such Truth in Tears

The baby cried,
Nobody came,
The mother had died,
In secret pain.

She'd overdosed,
Left him alone,
Lived out his last days,
No concern for him shown.

No knock on door,
He starved to death,
A child alone,
Took his last breath.

He followed her,
To the quiet place,
Pleading, ragged sobs stopped,
The neighbors' disgrace.

Where were those,
Who could've aided,
Heard the cries,
Time after time unabated?

Tall tale you say,
Could not be true,
But yet it was,
It made the news.

So turn the page,
Forget we read,
Of this heartbreak,
A child now dead.

Close now your ears,
Forget you heard,
Of the tragedy,
That once occurred.

Or can we now,
Be vigilant,
The challenge for us,
To protect the innocent.

Zoe Bonham (John Bonham)

The trip began as any other.
Something lovingly packed into a case,
for transport to another place.

The trip ended as any other.
Something lovingly packed into a case,
for transport to another place.

A doll's case, a coffin,
both containing a cold, flat, rigid form,
lid shut tightly against the light.

A doll's longsighted eyes to match your dad's,
eyes that look beyond, behind, or through you,
reflecting indefinite thoughts, mirroring the love from your
own eyes within theirs.

A doll's spun and woven hair,
to match the slander spun and woven of the father,
but it is only the father of lies defaming, if that's all that
you would hear.

While thirsting for the truth of his heart,
never drink from the spigot of muddy water,
filled with heavy metals that crush your spirit.

You missed him, always hoping that he would return,
his absence not annunciating a lack of love for you,
His hopes for you and your future
hinged on his current job.

The doll he bequeathed you,
Her mouth does not move,
but she speaks loudly of how much you were on his mind.
She represents the connection
sought across the distant miles.

If you bring her into the light,
you will see the truth.
Her mere presence disclosing all you need to know
to quench your soul.

Ocasek

Born against Hitlers might;
A polished scarecrow,
come to fight,
guarding against
crows' shallow, dull calling.
Mutt to Jeff,
metaphorical meters and lyrics surround
deep thrusting beat,
and organ's streamline flow.
A swirl of playful words,
taking you as deep as you'll go.
Thanks for bringing your shine
to music's hackneyed,
achromatic soundscape.
Red, white, and black aphrodisiac.
Goodbye, New Wave knight.

The Stone Man

The stone man, weak from chemo,
stood in front of the elevator doors.
Classic features on the beautiful face,
his frame and contours fragile.
If tipped over, he would break.

How I wish to have had
this statue in my home,
at another time,
before the craze and cracks were not so apparent.

But he is now beyond my reach to acquire,
and with that I am at peace,
for another art lover claims him,
and will add him to his collection.
And this collector, known to me,
will cherish the stone man
as much as I.

Freak
(For Laurie)

A small butterfly with niacin wings,
flits invited among the unwashed children of God
huddled in the hollow at McCree Park.

She darts among the many raps,
exchanges concerning love and hate,
right and wrong.
Palavers of good and evil,
the interchange of thoughts about weed or hash,
group-thinks deciding orange or blue.

On the ground,
her frame looks like a camel
with that humpback.
She teeters onto the scene using skeletal legs,
waving to all with spindly arms,
large blue eyes set deep
in the thinnest face ever seen,
a thatch of straw colored hair framing same.

When the great age of the water bearer became obsolete,
and the small window of acceptance closed,
and God's children scattered to the four corners,
then,
against the inexorable Ice Age,
emerging from the contrasting wind,
she,
so softhearted,
the one the laughing hyenas abused for great effect,
could bear no more,
She tore her own wings
in a desperate act of sorrow and anguished hopelessness.

Finally, eternally wretched,
when twilight's early black,
and the absolute pitch darkness
of the black twelfth consolidated,
she performed her final flight
taking to the air without benefit of chitin.
The beautiful, malformed freak,
who for a short time
had gained welcome to the family of man.

Moving Mountains

Now there will be
new and quite different stages to conquer,
fear, guilt, and useless bargains offered.
Guitars and ukes she puts aside to make room
for his failing body's needs.

A perfectly mapped out trail becomes an ancient pathway.
One trod by many, over centuries of time.
In spite of others' lack of success,
she will still fight the good fight,
although numb and wretched.

Backpacking up the mountain,
searching cures for his health's sake,
scrambling among the hard scrubbed brush,
moving weeds out of the way by herself,
hewing aside all sharp-edged blockades,
hoping, blood from hands mingling with tears.

That sky of God seen from so clear above
as she sings to him. Sweet Father, surely from here
my music suggests what dear peace
we need to make us whole again.
We have always together been on our way up.
My strong clear entreaty for closure is not meant
to suggest he has become inconvenient.
We need your healing melodic hymn to serenade us.

Today, He has answered with a refrain
intoned sweetly, sung from Heaven,
and let him enter the world of eternal music.
Now she's at the place where pitons do not matter.
One of them has fallen in the end.
She listens no longer for the ballad from the top,
taking this last descent alone.

Girl (for Nancy)

Boundless energy,
savagely made still,
memory snuffed,
its partner breath called down.
No way to calm
frantic what-ifs.
Like Tantalus,
relief forever out of reach,
for parents
of children whom death stole
by way of mortal hands.

Maestro
(Elegy for Wilbur)

The maestro raises his hand,
baton ready to strike the chord,
symphony forever unplayed.

In this watercolor world,
your round, elven look,
wide smile, crinkled eyes,
on an otherwise unlined face.

Symbolic sheaves of wheat,
among your progeny.
A freedom fighter legacy
left on a far shore.

Sounds not heard,
yet the oils of a Kansas son seen,
flowing across landscapes.
Still, quiet beauty,
panoramic, striking prairies.

An artist's mind, true heart,
your ready laugh
flows into the maestro's opus,
now silenced.
Yet not unheard by those who can dream.

Just Come Back

Not plates nor tools nor art from walls
Would I choose to remember you.
Please just come back and keep it all,
Not plates nor tools nor art from walls.
Your Will on which your name is scrawled,
Someone remove it from my view.
Not plates nor tools nor art from walls
Would I choose to remember you.

A Bluebird Sadly Flown
(A Tribute To A Pop Muse)

Edie,
born into a cage.
a bird wearing a feathered veil,
never pursuing tranquility.
A rolling stone of a woman,
sculptured in art and tailspins.
Publicly body untamed,
a privately tortured mind,
A break, a collapse,
at times,
her Cracks displayed to all,
coming unglued.
all her bluebirds finally came to roost.
Such a shame she never learned
how to land.

Zelda

A hyperactive extraterrestrial
with a silly name,
made us laugh and demonstrated
the tenderness that was man's hope.
Next, a teacher inspired a classroom of young men,
and millions of others
to pursue their knowledge of great literature.
A young father
warmed our hearts,
encouraged us to reach out
and embrace our families
from behind an old woman's façade.
We rooted for
a desperate widower,
as he searched for his heart's desire,
and cheered for him as he reached
the pinnacle of success,
his efforts finally rewarded.
Seymour Parrish creeped us out,
his obsession,
a sick psychological disorder,
more than just a lonely man
depicted here.

Teddy Roosevelt,
never seen as more human.
Leadership and longing
spurred him on
to help a community
of supernatural historical figures
understand the modern world.

Your dad,
acted in comedies and we were amused.
Played brave dramatic roles and we were awed.
Then, he hurt and suffered,
and we didn't listen as we should have.
It's too late to say to him,
Robin, we're sorry,
so, Zelda, we say it now to you.

John Gone Twice

John first left,
from a motorcade in Dallas.
His message of hope,
for prosperity for all,
interrupted.
The life of his wife
shattered in mere seconds
before her very eyes.

John next went away,
in front of The Dakota.
His message of hope,
for peace for all,
interrupted.
The life of his wife
shattered in mere seconds
before her very eyes.

Two distinct individuals,
both known around the world,
reflecting youthful energy,
realized and focus.
Taken too soon,
to this very day,
those who admired them
remain mournful at their passings,
and are not ashamed of it.

Bowie

Frail but unswerving,
His death unnerving,
If we'd begged him to stay, would he?
With pain and loss of dignity?
Now the Starman channels Lazarus,
Major Tom floats free to represent us.

The Search for Nimoy
February 27, 2015

Two-sided, multicultural extant
portrayed so well.
For most of that era's youth,
their first up - close exposure to biracial,
made more palatable by his representation.
Tolerance and acceptance became
as easy is blinking.

He, lead us to understanding
exotic possibilities,
inspired us to welcome,
to show interest and not spurn
something unique,
helping us see another world's peoples
as they possibly could be.

Sign of shin,
his yogic mudra
fashioned into a new symbol for peace.
Then a Vulcan phrase,
now part of our culture,
As familiar as
our own front door.

A heart made weak on Earth,
now throbs with distant life,
up and out, stellar, sparkling,
continuing, in a part of heaven
of which we cannot conceive.

He's now living again
in imagination's very essence,
where there's a negation of sorrow,
and fear has lost its purpose.

He taught us so well to face then
an unknown without anxiety.
Will we now continue his legacy,
and not quail?

Tommy Boy
(A Tribute to Petty)

Tommy Boy,
You've been called home.
That front porch light has flickered
on and off,
and thats your cue
to stop the strum and come inside.

Mama says
make sure to wash your hands,
and hang up your wings
before sitting down to supper.
But first, put that guitar away.
The time for playing is over,
as of today.

The Man in the Derby Hat

The man in the derby hat
hears his songbird tweeting
but it evokes no joy for him
because today is a dark day.

That's pronounced *de-pression*.

The man in the derby hat
walks the hills and villages
around where he lives
but it evokes no wonder in him.

Because today is a *gloomy* day.

All colors are dull.
Music and laughter are grating.
Food is tasteless
and the air is stale.

The man in the derby hat
sees the cliff
and decides that is
a good place from which to fly.
Like his songbird,
he sends his last tweet.

And.

The Unmoored

The ticking of the clock,
the snicking of the door,
the click of heels on hardwood floors.

The estate broker enters
to sell my neighbors' things.

Their obituaries having rested on the pages
of the city newspaper for several months.

His tools with which he built so much,
her bike she always planned to ride,

even things from bathroom cabinets,
nothing too sacred for prying eyes.

I choose a shirt from each,
to wear and remember
happier times with them.

It's nice to know
that while they no longer live on our street,
they have moved just a thought away.

May 14, 2015, the world lost a large part of its heart with the passing of Riley B. King, known to the world as B.B. Born on a cotton plantation called Berclair, he practiced guitar endlessly, later played live (brilliantly) more than that, and influenced an uncountable number of people. Gentle, hard working, talented, and generous, I named my newest guitar after him and wrote Berclair to honor him.

Linda Imbler, March, 2016

"I've said that playing the blues is like being black twice. Stevie Ray Vaughan missed on both counts, but I never noticed."

B. B. King

Berclair
(We Miss You, B.B. King)

Preach your way across the song,
Emotions, through music , acted on,
From tremolo to hypnotic dance,
Melancholy, moaning chant,
Feverishness without frenzy,
No jittery apology,
Love and loss intoned,
Hard hearted man or woman bemoaned,
Cheating man or woman disowned.

An army of scales and chords,
Bearing dissonant musical scores,
Playing the devils note, commanding legion,
Singing off the beat, syncopated strum,
A high-pitched piercing on the air,
Confront right or wrong on a dare,
Face up to the choice and tell,
Angels or demons, heaven or hell,
For having faced either allure
What else is there to fear?

Hear a heart sing, not rotten,
Only torn with grief and forgotten,
Feel the weight and vigor of this genre so aural,
Hear what's reflected in the sonic mural,
Elation, salaciousness, sensuality,
The mortal coil's gravity,
Call and response felt deep in skin and soul,
A beat strong and true, never growing cold,
The removal of scar inflicting yokes.

Warbling music of the gods
Rebellious enough to be outlawed
The good, the bad, take up either sword
Yet with other forms of song, blues is not at war
Merely disparate, or contrasting as such
Not the antithesis of other music much
A far cry from some, distant cousin of many
Distinctive and deviant, comparisons are plenty
But to find music incomparable to blues,
you won't find any.

Warm whiskey bellies on country lanes
Replaced by ice and snow in freezing veins
Some buoyancy as driven theater beats of Rock
Like heavy metal without angst or shock
No upbeat pop, optimistic with cheer
Just the human condition's atmosphere
Not Folk's eternal idealistic optimism
But its prism of fair minded liberalism
Its search for freedom matches heart
These descriptions explain, in part
The Blues enduring positivity
And Riley's eternal legacy.

Inge (Daginne)

The world is immensely diminished.

The beautiful lady-

with the sun in her hair,
the stars in her eyes,
and the enchantment of the moon
in her soul,

full of gratitude for time given.

She will become another

being,

light.

At second glance,

will she still be Dutch?

Or perhaps when she turns the corner,

Mescalero

or

Thai?

How inspiring that those with the biggest hearts

create the smallest distance

between each of us

and they keep the most luminous stars

in their eyes.

Tell the children

so that in latter years

they may watch for her.

Ripples On A Pond
(For Daniel)

One dead boy's circumstance should be confined
to the killer's here and now.

At least that's what the slayer hoped for.

After all, everyone should understand his need,
to have done what he did,
in the immediacy of the moment.

Here's the flaw in that logic:

That one dead boy, known to many,
loved by lots, respected by countless.

His loss affects legion in a multitude of ways.

Like ripples on a pond,
we feel the waves of the loss
spread out among us,
and these waves do not subside.

Jan

I had a friend who believed in Heaven.
A smart lady, who spoke with God.
She knew she was being heard.
Here, she had many abilities
and she was brave and feared little.

She had dabbled in magick,
lighting candles of different colors
and chanting over their flames
to bring about specific effects.
I never understood this behavior,
in parallel to her church-going ways.

She claimed that God's church
and the Kiowa teachings of her youth
and the Wiccan creeds were not at odds.
She said anything done on behalf of another,
if done with love, could not be a wrong thing.

We watched the sunsets in Key West
for several evenings in a row
while vacationing there.
She told me of her faiths
and her lack of fear about dying,
although at the time she did not know
that within a few years, that would be her reality.

I told her while she was ill
that she was facing it so bravely.
She smiled, as that seemed to please her.
I was not there for her last breaths,
but I suspect she literally heard God guiding her
that night.

I know she was speaking to him.

Jim Morrison

In the beginning,
he could speak in words and esoteric phrases
that explained all our strange days.

Near the end,
as his world spun sideways,
he no longer feared his visage
reflected from the whiskey bottle.

In the end, he morphed into some demented,
frustrated clown,
who claimed his name as its own.

At the final moment,
those creatures he spoke of so long ago
took him to the desert
and put him on the blue bus.

This is the end.

The Wise One

The shuffling, shanty limp way she moved,
The drag of loose skin under neck and eyes,
These things belied quickness of mind so wise,
Reminds me of someone whom I once loved.

What wisdom still lives in the tales of old wives?
Who do we turn to and when must we then turn?
Kingdoms crash while denying needful things learned,
Hard to reinvent wisdom in our lives.

The useful memory of ages reprised,
The potent apple a day or bright fish food,
Superstitious folklore, weird storytelling,
Our era better by common sense not denied.

She lives by the principled creeds of her youth,
This hunched yet lovely soul with smarts underused.
Though brittle bones and shaking hands might amuse
She shares with unselfish love what she learned as truth.

So I'll go and speak with her, but listen more,
Inhale the floral scent overlaid on old skin.
I want to hear knowledge that bears repeating,
At the way once shut, I'll throw open that door.

She taught me good things, gave much great sage advice,
Her keen wit and bright eyes reminding me now
Things told once by one I loved, I'd disavowed,
Things I must recollect and never leave behind.

Last Day

We got up so early with so much to do.
We made plans throughout the day,
separate events that would happen,
where our paths did not cross
and would keep us further apart.

We sent each other messages to voice
rather than answering the phone.
We chose not to meet for lunch
because we both wanted different foods that day.

We promised ourselves
to tell the other those loving words.
We bought each other a gift
but gave not of our time.

We chose to spend one precious hour
that evening in a heated debate
whose outcome neither could control.

Only one of us rose the next morning.

Tower of Bones

A parade seen
from the perspective
of the clavicles of a king among men;
or lengthy fields of farmland,
or guitarists on stage.
He counted train cars aloud to me as they passed.
Now as I stand at ground level,
and watch his funeral procession go by,
I long to once more
climb that tower of bones,
to view the majesty
of this life's moment,
while perched atop my father's shoulders.

Bequeathing

Decide the rhythms of your life,
never be a scourge,
Treat others well,
do not fear to love with courage,
Those left behind
will decide the tempo of your dirge.

Urn

I clutch tightly
your urned cremains.
If I put them down
you might disappear.
I put them in triple layered plastic bags
while I shower.
Strap them into the car seat
ever so snugly,
carry them into the store,
in that very large beach bag
that now serves as my purse,
when I can make myself buy food to eat.
At night, with you beside me,
I dream of our life together,
careful not to knock you off the bed,
to be scattered.
That I could not bear.
I recall the reasons I've loved you;
the magnitude of your heart
for all things living,
your capacity to forgive
both my naive foolishness and my purposeful
obstinacy,
your feverish defense of truth and justice.
There is much to cherish.
And while the way I am acting may seem strange,
there is a method to my madness.

If I hold this reliquary
close enough to me,
perhaps you will reappear.

A Message From Mom

Angels walk on Earth
in guise of mortal manifestation.
A painted rock with one word, love,
written on it and placed strategically
inside a zoo rock garden
by a kindly woman.
Found by a recently motherless boy.
His thought,
my mother left this for me.
Through heat of summer
or chill of winter,
children will remind us
that those who left us leave messages,
if only we act with the eyes and ears
of our early years,
and we look and we listen with the hearts
of the innocent.

Last Summer in Galveston

And you asked me
to walk along the sandy shores
in bare feet,
and I complained about the hot, summer sand
burning my soles.
And if, in another season,
something happened to you,
I would walk on hot coals
to bring you back.

And you asked me
to get in the water,
and I complained
that I could not see the ocean's bottom.
And if, in another season,
something happened to you,
I would endure jellyfish stings
to bring you back.

Now another season is here.
You asked for such small things.
How I wish I could re-answer that past summer!

Because

Telephone

He tried listening to her
breathing as he sat beside her
hospital bed,
knowing it grew shallower
each passing second,
but what he heard
was the ringing
which drove forward those
memories of her.

He remembers her
wiping the countertop
and telling him
to return the ketchup
bottle to its rightful place
on the second shelf,
as he teased of not
remembering where it belonged.
He would call her when he got to work,
ask her if it was still
in the same place,
nice and safe with the
other egg products,
a shared laugh each morning.

He recalls the
teapot in the kitchen,
he could hear
the water running to
refill it while she filled his head
with the gossip
of the day.
Those small pieces of minutia
she scattered around his
mind like bird seed
for him to peck at
while he ate his evening meal,
hearing new
sound bytes,
ones he had not heard
when he called her
from his desk at noon while
he ate his lunch,
asking,
what was the
news of the morning?
Recalls the last time
he used the
phone to call for help,
to get her here; knowing there's
just one more call she will answer.

Upon the Shore

A stooped man stands on the shore,
looks out to sea,
feels gravity strengthen its grip,
such tired days are these.
He sees beyond the horizon,
imagines a face in the clouds,
lined,
yet still beautiful and compelling,
beauty unmatched by any.
He feels the stir of his heart,
the fluttering, lightening sensation
allowed to all who love.
This brief moment in time,
having passed all too quickly,
will have to sustain him,
as he now turns turns his eyes
away from the sky,
and searches for the path leading home.

Declaration

When I am old,
And called across the sea,
And beauty, peace, and ecstasy unfold,
Make no sad laments for me.

A quiet shore awaits,
Those long passed, I'll meet again,
Within majestic open gate,
The happiest I'll ever be.

I'll walk the pathway,
Abounding sights,
Shoreline blue and silver gray,
Days and nights now finite.

And when you come,
And call and look for me,
Follow the silence to my sanctum,
On the shore along the sea.

Babies

They marched into cities,
 countrysides and parks,
 streaming into towns,
 across the globe.

They weren't supposed to be here,
they'd been dispatched,
but they weren't standing for it,
and so they came back.

All the babies,
unwanted and cast aside,
now coming into their own,
their time has come.

Now we must find a place for them,
they won't leave again.
They know they are owed,
for what was done to them,
over centuries of time.

Ripped and torn,
before being born,
reparation overdue,
pay them with our own blood,
theirs already shed.

Man in the Bath

In this dark harbor,
a tsunami reveals its strength,
quickly,
without mercy.
Later, the partially submerged empty vessel
rocks back-and-forth,
knocking against pilings
with a constant, monotonous
rhythm reminiscent of a stranger's knock on the
door.
This asylum,
still shrouded in darkness,
newly coated with red algae bloom,
lies in wait,
for what, it's not known.
The harbormaster
has already visited and departed.
The rhythm of the knocking slows,
as at once,
this shelter becomes alit.
The air is stirred,
and so begins
the shriek of the first gull
as the vision of what lies here
is illumined.

Pinned

Such a game,
Line up the ball with the arrows,
It spins along the lane,
Knock them down,
A spare, a spare,
Must try again,
Strike, strike, strike,
Boom, they all fall down.
Line up the ball with the sight,
It spins above the classroom floor,
Knock them down,
A spare, a spare,
Spare no one,
Must try again,
Strike, strike, strike,
Boom.
They all
Fall
Down.

Small Detail

Here he is
on the ground,
this small detail,
right outside the periphery of those
who step over him,
recognizing an object,
some small detail
there underfoot,
yet at the moment, a minutia,
insignificant,
in the midst of broadcasting
blasts and explosions.
Line of sight raised straight ahead
or to either side,
where detonations are heard and felt,
and steal first position
for what the senses embrace.
Small details,
tiny figures,
lost in the display of conflagration seen.
The pungency of sulfur smelled.
The small details,
the greatest victims of any conflict,
for there are bigger fish to fry.
The small details,
the largest casualties of warfare.
So they lie.

Bells Ringing

All around us,
bells are ringing,
heralding
the new dawn to come.

Soldiers on all ships
coming home.
More,
in flight returning.
War has been fought,
and the end has been arbitrated.

This last war,
mankind, as a whole, now victorious,
deciding to celebrate freedom
across all lands.

Each person adjudicated,
with all scores settled,
a covenant of peace
to harmonize this sphere.

And those in crypts,
though they be dead,
release the hopeful breath they have held
for so very long and join the gleeful celebration.

Final Count

The final count,
after the conflict,
of those left standing.
A sum of hollow, empty vessels,
not feeling the aftermath,
for the souls of the dead
carried the souls of the survivors
away with them when they took flight.

The final count
of those left standing,
looking beyond the carnage,
no longer able to imagine
what man once built
in that place where he dwelt,
constructed by desire and philosophy.

The final count
of those left standing,
the absolute scorecard designed
to identify the victors,
when all bloodshed and hostility cease,
those left standing,
declared the heirs to triumph,
and to them is bequeathed desolation.

Have You Heard The Butterflies Sing?
(Vietnam)

Have you heard the butterflies sing?
Rolling the quiet skies with beating wings,
Dropping men with olive green helmets from the sky,
Rocket's red glare not ceasing.

Have you heard the butterflies cry?
Like the roar of lions and panthers
At pride's decline,
Watching those same men on the ground as they die.

Have you heard the butterflies grieve?
Guttural, pleading rotors,
Leaving troops cemented to the ground,
There's nothing left for them to retrieve.

Have you heard the butterflies fall?
Silenced by jungle fire
Against the clipping of wings,
Metallic wreckage in awkward sprawl.

Butterflies scream the same as men,
Caught in a circle of human torment.
When will we learn to circumvent
So much human blood being spent?

Intended King Most Deadly

One man kills one man,
sets in motion
the falling of nations, empires.
Each taking sides.
Ideologies questioned, defended, defeated.
Four years of death,
destruction most terrible,
a bitter ending,
yet also, the beginning of something
so heinous 21 years out.

One century later,
still deep wounds that will not heal,
trusts that cannot be regained,
peace not to be seen between some.

All because one man killed not one man,
but 16 million or more.

Tolling

Wheels fast spun, life undone,
the lemming crowd of cars, the fleet
with pedal to the metal.
Racing, each to be the first,
metallic he-beasts
making passes at cute Cougars, Chrysler's, Cadillacs.

Toll taken at the end of the road,
before that, the rotating wheels grab the ground,
sounds the alarm
at the rumble strips,
like drum fire,
warning to slow down
along the asphalt.

But rolling thunder
so loud -i s jeering,
steering and veering
around,
without fearing.
I'm hearing
that the death knell is now ringing.

Ahead,
the tolling of that bell is the final sound.

Now pay the toll.

Death was heralded,
and tall, modern cairns are constructed
from blood and mangled metal.
The lemming city stream of cars
races past the also-rans and their monuments,
and sounds the alarm
at the rumble strips
like drum fire.

Celebrating A Death

A new rain falls upon the earth,
Rain of tears from happy eyes,
No more storm in bone or blood,
Soft stream at cancer's demise.
That bane of bone and blood and organ,
What once tore down with drenching rage,
Now to be far memory.
Behold festive great events,
Glad hearts congratulate,
Sorrow replaced with exultation,
Smiles no longer fade.
Planetary jubilee,
Across this orb once held hostage,
Triumph cheered across boundaries,
Raise a glass, have a dance,
Celebrate the healing rain.

Burying My Cat

The storm raged and left,
so the forest ground is soft.
I imagine all the bones
to be found in five year's time.
But, I always knew
he did not want to be dead,
and as his meows
echo through the air,
I am called to follow him
to our mutual end.

Schadenfreude

The crows refuse to turn
away from the carnage.
The broken and bent frames
of machine and man
thrill them.

Across the road is spilled
dreams and desires,
never to be realized,
and the crows flap their wings
with glee.

Taurus of Man
(An Ekphrastic Poem)

Neither lit lamp nor prayer replace this dark
exhibition of a graveyard.
Alas, Guernica, tongues as sharp pieces,
sharp shattered shards of broken blades.

An eye-shaped bulb does not the red reflect
two-fisted grips of death-like hands.
Alas, Guernica, hands with monstrous bent,
sharps caused by strafing fusillade.

Winds of war and arrows blown through
windows.
Bull's tail drawn as arm of the dead.
Long necks neighbor faces beyond salvation,
art - black, white, and gray shows what's been
slayed.

The Taurus of Man shown in pen and ink
depicting his need to conquer.
His stubborn belief that he's meant to fight war.
Eyes askew - agony forever displayed.

Dead Clocks

All the dead clocks
stilled through the ages.
Their silence lies
among the cacophony of busyness.

Days that continue,
things to be done,
sound and movement
surrounding them.

Yet they lie still,
generations,
representing their own time,
the back when,
the before.

And their hearts no longer tick.

Beyond

Homeless Souls

When God forgives Lucifer,
and all of Hell is emptied,
when the entry doors to that fetid place
are closed and locked forever,
what will happen to the still unrepentant?

The Master said the poor shall always be with us,
so shall it also be with those who continue
to want to hate, to hurt.
Though fallen angels become sorry and bewail,
the morally bankrupt will feel no need
for such banal sensibilities.

What realm will then welcome these,
the virtuously destitute,
dishonorable barbarous wicked beasts,
committing the basest of acts
to the detriment of all worlds?

What realm will then welcome these?
When all talk of hope or justice
have no notice taken by their deaf ears,
the uncaring ears of the iniquitous,
homeless for all time.

What Once Was Once Was There

Is there any place on earth,
within 100 yards of where you now stand,
where someone has not died?
In all the millennia of existence,
how many times have the living trespassed
over unseen graves of those
who have perished?

Do we ever remember they existed,
since no marker reminds us?
Do we even offer a prayer
to the well-being of their spirits?
Especially for those who had
no one to mourn them long ago.
Was their life any less
notable or commemorative
than those who,
by someone, were missed?

As sad as this may sound,
do not forget that not all peoples
spend eternity in the ground.
Sky or cliff burials, cremation,
these ways matter to some.

Whether or not they chose
their own underground internment,
memorialize the buried dead,
those you've violated,
where and when you can,
even if you did not know them,
and thereby let trespass seem not so delinquent.

Cousin May

I tell St. Peter at the gate,
one of my major regrets is still not atoned.
Now's the time to make it right.

May's stumble and fall onto the dirt road,
for two children in a car watching through the window,
became banana peel hilarity.
For the adults present and close,
a great cause for concern, of the bloody nose,
stanched by only the greatest effort.

Within a few months, her angel escorts left with her,
never to let her fall again.
She stepped into eternity,
not ever having said an unpleasant word to any
nor leveling any accusations to them.

Although she did not learn of our transgression,
I must tell her I'm sorry.
This shall be my testimony
to the spiritual evolution of my soul
from one end of my life to the other.

I ask St. Peter at the gate
to please entreat her to come meet me.
Now's the time to make it right.

Chester

Chester ran across the road,
or tried to.
He didn't quite make it.
Here comes running
the one who neither believed
in licenses nor leashes.

A truth as hard as the concrete
across which Chester is now spilled,
entering her mind,
as tears of remorse
release the other way.

Then Chester stands,
once again whole,
without blood-soaked fur.
He gives himself a quick shake
and runs on,
runs like the wind.
Nothing's gonna stop him
in his new world.

Last Train

The railroad tracks sound as the rattle of castanets.
Do we dare clip-clop over the bones of our kin?
That stretch of track
that only the ticketed may ride,
Yellow lanterned men at the sides,

Guiding

Like Charon with his lamp
Leading us across the Rubicon,

Or a reflection off of St. Michael's sword.

There's a station up ahead,
We'll know in a minute.

Ascension

Climb the wall of eternity
with pitons formed from undone deeds,
backpack filled with words in like manner unspoken,
and ropes still tied to human arms outstretched.
At the apex,
leave all behind
except that one memory,
which you are allowed to carry
throughout your transmigration.

The Ma'am in the Moon

When I walk through that final door,
I long to step onto the surface
of a blood red moon,
where all the Earth's new days' promises
and passing days' done deeds
can only be observed
by those who still breathe.
This declaration of humanity's best intents,
even unto the last sliver of light.

May I romp on for all time,
floating joyfully from peak to peak,
exploring the nethermost depths of each crater,
polishing rocks as I go.
My smile paramount to the light given off
by this celestial orb of night,
to be seen by the children of all places,
for these are the souls that must be inspired.

And someday young stargazers
might look upon this spectacular rock,
their hearts swelling with brighter assurance,
prompting a genesis of future, earnest purpose
for healing the world,
And call to mom, call to dad,
come and look, come and see,
the beautiful lady
on the beautiful blood red moon tonight.

War is Dead

There's an odd place in an alternate dimension,
where all wars are fought with skeletons.

These subjects of osteology lie dormant until conscription,
well preserved in the interim.

Adults only, minors never get to be
heroic revenants, noble bones.

Once wakened, they are fully conscious of their purpose,
realizing that the burden and horrors of war
have been put on their ossified cages only.

They, without souls, but not without honor,
the fleshed never harmed as these bony frames battle
with bow and arrow, sticks and stones, knife and spear.

All this,
for the same reasons inhabitants
destroy themselves on other worlds.

Wolves In Sheep's Clothing

Folks wearing somber colored clothes
with somber faces,
wishing to be elsewhere.
Unease curls around them like the mist
rising from between the stones
through which they navigate.
Cold, still, silent cairns, under which
perhaps some other lonely, rejected outcasts now lie.
Those left howling,
by others too busy
to hear the deep hurt endured
with each passing friendless day.
Now they stand,
dry eyed, dutiful.
They are here because
even a pretentious display counts.
Appearing atop the nearby hill,
one lone Wolf,
he throws back his head and cries.
At once he stills,
lowers his head,
matching the grim lowering of what
will not return.

Spoiled Fruit

It was hard to confront that black banana.
My days away from home had changed the shape
and I'm sure the taste.
The other fruits looked no better.
All were dried and shrinking fast.
but, there'd been no time for the fridge.
And as his skin will now follow the way of the fruit,
the idea of spoiled fruit and a now spoiled life
is still too much to bear.

Part of Me

That part of me
you took when you left.
Those pieces of me I gave you.
Hold on to them.
Keep them close to you
until we have the chance to meet by and by.
They will be safe,
with you, in your quiet haven below,
inside your wooden ark you alone inhabit.
Possessed with loving qualities,
those gifts will keep memory of me alive.
I don't miss what I bequeathed to you.
I know they're not gone forever,
only lent and held,
as you lie sleeping, waiting for my knock.
The best parts of me borrowed for a time
while you wait. I gave you my love,
I gave you my peace,
knowing where you were,
alone, you would need them.

The Looking

The woman
newly become as wraith
walks among the stones,
lost, yet looking
for something she vaguely remembers.

The dimming day looks as the same,
this oncoming night, resembling many long past.

What she wishes to find does not come easily to her
mind,
yet is all consuming on her psyche.

The weight on her heart is painful,
but she must continue,
for once she sights it, she will have tranquility,
after so much searching.

So she seeks, seeks, seeks…..

Ah, there it is,
in the ground.
So common looking
like all the others.
Yet, this one is special,
because of him.
And she digs and digs down into the earth,
knowing she will once more finally touch him.

50 years of searching,
and then she takes him into her arms.
This tiny thing,
once again to love him as before.

Long Strange Trip

As he pays her passage
into the next leg of the journey,
as the sun sets behind her eyes one minute
and rises in the next,
she thinks to herself,
what a long, strange trip it's been.

The depot affords a beckoning sideview
of Morrison's blue bus,
all board but she,
until the last second.
A memorable ride,
for never had she met so many interesting people,
and kindness the very essence of them.

Debarking upon arrival,
mysteriously once again alone,
she thinks to herself,
what a long, strange trip that was.

She had packed up her hopes and dreams,
legacies for the future,
in wills and trusts while earthbound.
Now no need for baggage of any kind
on this wondrous long, strange trip.

And here at the terminus,
familiar faces,
full of laughter and joy.
She thinks to herself,
I am glad to finally return home
from the long, strange trip.

Bus in Heaven

If you spot the sun from the bus window,
that large sphere is resolutely yellow.
Repentance and forgiveness now aligned.
The blessed dream here,
while the damned languish elsewhere.
There is no end to the soul.
Eden was once within our grasp,
now paradise comes full circle-
the perfect turn.

The elegance of cold skin,
and the scent of myrrh,
ripe among us.

We may recover that great garden,
yet again.

Poe's Annabel Lee

Dearly departed,
your face fitted inside the ornate filigree frame.
Your feathered hat
surrounds a rawboned face.
Your shoulders hold a filmy wrap of satin and lace.
Your skeletal fingers
shift in the light on graceful hands.
Velvet gloves clasped as you, the lost lover,
endure your woeful waiting,
as the pendulum wall clock ticks,
and you hoard his books,
as you anticipate
his arrival.

When I Find You Again (Barefoot Dreams)

I'm running as fast as I can to catch up.
And, when I'm finally even with your pace,
I can throw off my running shoes
and go with you.
We can swim with sharks that won't bite.
Climb,
to the very tops of mountains,
and not fall.
Sleep outside in the rain,
and never fear the lightning that accompanies it.
We can do it all,
and nothing can hurt us.
We will finally walk barefoot,
arm in arm,
throughout eternity.

The Storyteller Within the Blue Latitudes

My mind is sharp, and oddly enough,
I can see in all directions at the same time.
People's mouths move, but there is no sound.
I rather enjoy not having to breath.
The air seems, well, cleaner somehow.

After all the illness and pain,
I've taken a turn for the better,
and I'm doing quite well.

My unblinking eyes are easy on the lenses.
The memory of what is overhead is fading rapidly.
I stroll through my thoughts,
my body chooses to remain still inside this vault.

Being dead is a solitary exercise,
and I do so relish my solitude.

The firmament becomes obscured,
and I repose in state happily ever after.

SOULS

Conversation

Justice spoke to Death
Asking when to intervene.
Death replied,
"At all times,
For you have seen
What I have seen."

One Man's Karma

The dead man sits in the small room
without sustenance or light.
There are no books or windows.
He cannot speak, yet even if he could,
there is no one with whom to do so.

The only things he has been given
are his memories,
strong, vivid.
The only time he leaves this place
is when his soul enters another's body
at the height of their fear and agony.
He leaves again
at the moment of their peaceful death,
returns back here to relive
what suffering has just occurred.
So many instances;
A black man lynched in Alabama,
An old Vietnamese woman torched alive in a hut,
A blind, one legged, starving Kabul child
stepping on a land mine,
A Detroit three-year-old gunned down
by cross-fire while playing in the front yard,
A small, terrified terrier
being used for bait in a dog fight,
A 911 plane passenger,
Syria,
Koalas caught in Australian bushfires.

The karmic wheel spins for him,
never slows, ticks off each offense,
holds no grudge,
just reflects what is due to him.
It's scary how relentless and unforgiving
this wheel is to this man.
Wherever there is evil,
he has no power over it.
It controls him
as he relives the horrors of others,
even beyond madness.
It's happening again.
He knows it's time.
The voice calls to him,
"Adolph, come."

Dead Poets and the Lugubrious Living

Dead poets' poems,
seen within the admiring eyes of the living.
The power of sadness penned,
employing language, graceful
liquidity. Poets who wept their anguish
upon paper's haven, suffering
laid out in words, using their fingers
as feet to take journeys of misfortune
and delight.

Deceased poets, once walking in another world,
held today in great regard by bootless extants.
Dead poets dotting the skies,
the seas, and the landscapes of books,
filled long ago with universal messages
traveled across time, to speak to
the equally wistful living.

Intermission

Good, kind Tim died on Tuesday,
He should've ended right there,
But the faeries didn't want him yet,
His soul just floated on the air.

He landed in the lost land of Oolmuk,
Where angels and demons coexist,
It was a pleasant sensation to be in a place,
Where fear, loneliness and hatred aren't missed.

And here among such entities,
He dwelt for many years,
When at last he felt caged, and he raged,
And he cursed the Divine through his tears.

My Soul is so tired, my strength is so spent,
My thoughts are confused, I wish you'd relent,
And let me sleep the sleep of those who have felt,
That they have been honest and productive
with the hand they were dealt.

So he asked the question,
Entreated to his God,
To truly rest must I worship you or just truly love others?

So kneeling he prayed for rest and freedom,
And at last real death befell him,
And his new parents celebrated,
The rebirth of good, kind Tim.

Tomb

Indian empress
in majestic palace.
Pharaoh,
colossal pyramids and valley of kings.
Chinese emperor
under protection of enormous, imperial army.
Abbeys and churches,
splendid, kingly.
Czech ossuary,
decorative bones create glorious ambiance.
Immense Irish mounds,
green and grand.
Parisian and Italian catacombs,
lambent flames of candles illuminating.
Monuments to presidents and monarchs,
visited by heads of state.
Tomb of the Unknown Soldier
represents otherwise forgotten victims of wars
past and present.
City cemeteries,
vaults and mausoleums dot the landscape.
Family graveyards,
tombstones detail ancestral history.
Solitary, unmarked graves
on purpose or not.
Mass graves,
one of the spoils of war.

A small, dark grotto,
once covered with a rolling rock,
Now empty.
Its former resident
watches over them all
from his vantage point,
watches over the living
and the still entombed.

List of Poetry Journals/Magazines Where My Poems First Appeared

First appeared in *Setu Bilingual Journal:*
"Dream's Garden"

First appeared in *Poetry Quarterly:*
"Time"
"The Unmoored"

First appeared in *Fine Flu Journal:*
"Atop The Hill"

First appeared in *Broad River Review:*
"Beautiful Ruin"

First appeared in *Highland Park Poetry:*
"Fortress As Duet In Latter Days"

First appeared in *Orange Blush Zine:*
"Winter's Witches"

First appeared in *Foliate Oak Literary Review:*
"The De-evolution of Bandaids"

First appeared in *Scarlet Leaf Review:*
"Chronology"
"The Cards Spoke"
"The First Week Of Shattered Dreams"
"Wings"
"If Only"

First appeared in *Beneath The Rainbow:*
"Moment"

First appeared in *Bindweed:*
"The Heart's Camera"

First appeared in *PPP Ezine:*
"Déjá Vu"
"The Ticking Of Winter's Clock"

First appeared in *Mad Swirl:*
"Digging The Day"

First appeared in *The Beautiful Space - A Journal Of Mind, Art, and Poetry:*
"The Forgotten Life Of Velma Hopkins"

First appeared in *The Writer's Magazine:*
"Dennys At Midnight"

First appeared in *Door=Jar:*
"Paper Dolls Left In The Rain"

First appeared in *The Blue Nib:*
"Michael's Memories"
"Egghead Knew Best"
"In Bare Feet"
"Six Feet"
"Inge (Daginne)"
"Last Day"
"Last Train"

First appeared in *Tropica Laced:*
"Bonham, Texas"

First appeared in *The Unbroken Journal:*
"Futuristic Farm"
"The Looking"

First appeared in *Mused: Bella Online:*
"Footsteps That Have Long Faded"

First appeared in *Free Lit Magazine:*
"Summer Vacation Memories '66"

First appeared in *Piker Press:*
"Polaroid"
"Dead Clocks"

First appeared in *Medusa's Kitchen:*
"Painted Walls"
"Chester"

First appeared in *Ariel Chart:*
"Before The Sand Stops"
"The Gift of Myrrh"
"As Alice Said, I Love The Dead"
"A Bluebird Sadly Flown (A Tribute To A Pop Muse)"
"Tommy Boy (A Tribute To Tom Petty)"
"Ripples On A Pond"
"Schadenfreude"
"Spoiled Fruit"
"Dead Poet's And The Lugubrious Living"

First appeared in *Basil O'Flaherty:*
"Night Guard"

First appeared in *Corvus Review:*
"Gossips"

First appeared in *Impspired:*
"Flight"

First appeared in *Buck Off Magazine:*
"Hands"

First appeared in *Poetry Online:*
"Berclair"

First appeared in *Madness Muse Press:*
"Jim (Morrison)"

First appeared in *Boned:*
"Tower Of Bones"

First appeared in *Anapest Journal:*
"Urn"
"Declaration"

First appeared in *Anti-Heroin Chic:*
"A Message From Mom"

First appeared in *Bluepepper:*
"Man In The Bath"
"One Man's Karma"

First appeared in *Dead Snakes:*
"Pinned"
"Small Detail"

First appeared in *The Poet Magazine:*
"Final Count"
"Have You Heard The Butterflies Sing?"

First appeared in *Black Poppy Review:*
"Burying My Cat"

First appeared in *Dual Coast:*
"Taurus Of Man"

First appeared in *Aulos Anthology:*
"Bus In Heaven"

First appeared in *Quail Bell:*
"Poe's Annabel Lee"

First appeared in *GloMag:*
"When I Find You Again (Barefoot Dreams)"

First appeared in *Be Happy Zone:*
"Tomb"